Praise for John O'Leary and *In Awe*

"Awe comes naturally to children. Somewhere en route to adulthood, we lose it. John O'Leary's engaging new book encourages us to see the world through a child's eyes, and in doing so, rediscover its wonder."

—Mitch Albom,
New York Times bestselling author of *Finding Chika*

"When it comes to energy and optimism, John O'Leary never takes a day off. He is absolutely 'game on' every moment, and his enthusiasm is contagious. His passion for life drips from every page of *In Awe,* so get ready to have your world rocked—and to lose every excuse for staying mired in whatever rut has you stuck."

—Dave Ramsey,
bestselling author and nationally syndicated radio show host

"John O'Leary is the perfect man to help us unleash inspiration, meaning, and joy in our lives, as he does for others every day of his life."

—Brian Buffini,
chairman and founder of Buffini & Company

"Life-giving: That is the most accurate description of *In Awe*. Once again, John O'Leary manages to reach us right where we are with this book and inspire us in ways very few others have ever done. John's uncanny ability to tell emotionally moving stories not only shifts our perspective so we see hope in ourselves, but he masterfully highlights our commonalities so we see hope in each other. *In Awe* is important and timely for the times we live in. *In Awe* has the power to revive the world's long-lost joy. Every human being needs this book."

—Rachel Macy Stafford,
New York Times bestselling author of *Hands Free Mama*

"Do you remember the last time you were fascinated by something most people consider ordinary? How old were you when it happened? John O'Leary's new book shows the reader how to regain the excitement for life that many of us are not even aware we have lost. *In Awe* is a book I needed."

—Andy Andrews,
New York Times bestselling author of *The Traveler's Gift*

"If the greatest advantage in this life is a positive brain, it is vital we find a way to bring joy back into our work and relationships. John O'Leary shows us that joy and awe can not only be recaptured, they must be. They are the fuel we use to face a challenging and complicated world with boldness and confidence. Reading *In Awe* will return hope and wonder to your pursuit of happiness."

—Shawn Achor,
New York Times bestselling author of *The Happiness Advantage*

"My career and passion is to wake individuals and organizations to their full potential. John O'Leary does exactly that in the book *In Awe*. He'll remind you of the natural joy, hope, and wonder you possessed as a child, explain why you lost it, and reveal how you can return to it. Read this book. Thank me later."

—Hal Elrod,
bestselling author of *The Miracle Morning*

"In a world full of negativity, John O'Leary will remind you that you always have a choice. Life is still good and the best days remain ahead. This is a must-read. You'll be *In Awe* at how John changes your outlook and at the possibilities you will see still present in your life."

—Mel Robbins,
host of *The Mel Robbins Show* and bestselling author of *The 5 Second Rule*

"We all know the attitude we choose determines the lives we live. But I can think of few people who model this better than John O'Leary. After reading *In Awe,* you'll be inspired to not only choose a positive attitude but to embrace the gift of daily joy and live a life of meaning. With so much negativity and divisiveness in the world, the time is now to return to living *In Awe*."

—Jon Gordon,
#1 bestselling author of *The Energy Bus*

"If you, like me, fell in love with John O'Leary's heart through the story of his personal journey, this book will only extend your admiration. John reminds us all to hit pause, to reflect on and to appreciate the life we are blessed with. I'm an even bigger fan of his after reading *In Awe*."

—Don Yaeger,
eleven-time *New York Times* bestselling author

IN AWE

IN AWE

Rediscover Your CHILDLIKE WONDER to
Unleash INSPIRATION, MEANING, and JOY

JOHN O'LEARY

WITH CYNTHIA DITIBERIO

CURRENCY

NEW YORK

Published in the United States by Currency, an imprint of
Random House, a division of Penguin Random House LLC, New York.

CURRENCY and its colophon are trademarks of Penguin Random House LLC.

LIBRARY OF CONGRESS CATALOGING-IN-PUBLICATION DATA
Names: O'Leary, John, author.
Title: In awe / John O'Leary.
Identifiers: LCCN 2020003070 (print) | LCCN 2020003071 (ebook) |
ISBN 9780593135440 (hardcover) | ISBN 9780593135457 (ebook)
Subjects: LCSH: Wonder. | Curiosity. | Children. | Joy.
Classification: LCC BF575.A9 O44 2020 (print) | LCC BF575.A9 (ebook) |
DDC 814/.6—dc23
LC record available at https://lccn.loc.gov/2020003070
LC ebook record available at https://lccn.loc.gov/2020003071

Printed in the United States of America on acid-free paper.

currencybooks.com

9   8   7   6   5   4   3   2   1

First Edition

To the little ones who ensured my life
would never be the same.

Jack, Patrick, Henry, and Grace:

Because of you, I am more daring,
more loving, and more alive.

Let this book remind you always
of all you taught me and how much I love you.

And, my children, as the years pass and you forget
to live these lessons yourself,

let this book remind you to reclaim
what remains possible within you.

———

On the night you were born,

the moon smiled with such wonder

that the stars peeked in to see you

and the night wind whispered,

"Life will never be the same."

—Nancy Tillman,
On the Night You Were Born

Contents

INTRODUCTION

Raise Your Hand

IT IS OUR CHOICES, HARRY, THAT SHOW WHAT WE TRULY
ARE, FAR MORE THAN OUR ABILITIES.

**J. K. Rowling, *Harry Potter* and
*the Chamber of Secrets***

The auditorium was buzzing.

As a speaker, I've had the pleasure of presenting to organizations around the world, from Southwest Airlines to Microsoft; from twenty thousand salespeople at a national sales conference to a dozen CEOs in a boardroom.

On this day, I looked forward to talking with one of my favorite audiences: school-age kids. I love their voices, their laughter, their zest. I always leave the room energized and reminded of how lit up for life our little ones can be.

School districts typically invite me to speak to their entire school, but divide students into several groups based on age. First I get the pleasure of speaking to the youngest cohort, grades one through three. And let me tell you, it's obvious as soon as they enter the auditorium: The party's on.

Laughter bounces off the walls, smiles beam from faces, energy is high, and voices are loud. When I ask questions during my presentation, they answer heartily; when it is their turn for questions, they wave hands in the air in the hope of being called on. When it is time to return to class, they leap to their feet, a line forms by the door, and they fist-bump me excitedly as they prance on to the next part of their day.

One of the boys in this group pulled back in shock after giving me a fist bump. He looked at my right hand. Then my left. He stared into my eyes, held my gaze, and asked as if stunned, "What happened to your hands, mister?"

Okay. I'd just shared the story of what happened to my hands. I had literally just stood in front of this boy and his classmates and explained: I'd made a huge mistake. Blown up my house when I was nine. Set myself on fire. Damaged my body. Lost my fingers to amputation. But my life was still filled with possibility, and so was theirs. I was expected to die. But I beat the odds. Impossible miraculous things still happened. Every day.

Had he missed the presentation? Been stuck in the bathroom? Was the microphone not on?

Whatever the cause, I took a slice of humble pie, bent to his level, and responded, "Well, when I was nine years old, I was in a house fire. I lost my fingers, but am doing awesome today."

I could see him thinking about it for a moment, trying to make sense of this, before replying, "Oh my gosh!" He continued enthusiastically, "We had a speaker earlier today, and when he was nine years old he was burned in a house fire, too." After a short pause he added, "You two should meet!"

The little boy then extended his hand, gave me a fist bump, and skipped down the hallway.

I shook my head and laughed.

Kids may sometimes get the answers wrong, but they are unafraid to ask questions, even the hard ones.

I was still smiling to myself when the next group showed up.

Grades four through six are more subdued. There's a little less noise when they enter, fewer hands elevated when it's time for questions, not as much excitement as they filter out of the auditorium.

Then, grades seven and eight enter. Eventually the high school students. And with each subsequent group—well, you can guess what happens, right?

Heads are down. Phones are in hand. During the presentation fewer answers are offered, hardly any questions asked. They're great kids and are internalizing the message, but it seems they've outgrown the joy of fully participating.

It's easy to blame it on adolescence. Sure, you could fault their hormones, their surly attitudes, their desire to fit in, or their craving to be cool.

And yet, is the way they participate so different from the manner in which we show up as adults?

Think about it.

When was the last time you waltzed into a room buzzing with energy?

When was the last time you showed up to a presentation convinced it was going to be awesome?

When was the last time you responded to a question by waving your hand in the air, begging to be called on, shouting out the answer?

We've transformed from excited, engaged, wildly optimistic kids who sprint to school into disengaged, distracted, cynical adults with most of that enthusiasm snuffed out.

Maybe we claim it's because we now possess the wisdom of experience. We've been around the block and know that life isn't always easy. In fact, it's often downright hard.

We're sprinting on the treadmill of doing more and more with fewer resources and less time. We're exhausted, don't feel we are getting anywhere, and tired of all the effort. The constant negativity broadcast through news outlets and social media has us convinced the best days are behind us and the end is near. Don't believe me? Watch your evening news tonight for validation. You're doomed!

Although we're more connected digitally and living in closer proximity to one another than at any point in the history of the world, we've never felt more isolated and alone. It's negatively affecting every generation, but showing up most dramatically in young adults, with 30 percent of millennials reporting that they feel lonely, and 22 percent admitting they have no friends.[1]

I don't know about you, but I think it's time we address how we are approaching life so we can get back to living lit up, excited and inspired for what's ahead.

And I think our kids have the answers.

This book is an invitation to reawaken five essential senses that you possessed as a child that will allow you to get back in touch with what it is like to live with the whimsical freedom and intrinsic joy of children waltzing through life.

It was a time when you were insanely curious, and your inquisitive nature refused to believe anything was impossible.

When you stepped into every experience with eyes wide open, heart brimming with hope, expecting amazing things.

When you were totally immersed in the moment, instead of worried about the past or anxious about the future.

When you weren't concerned about how you appeared to others and approached everyone (even total strangers) as potential friends.

When you stepped in boldly, raised your hand high, and felt the invigorating sense of freedom that allows you to go all in, dare greatly, and inhabit your life fully.

I call this living In Awe.

This is our true nature.

Unfortunately, as we age, this natural state erodes as the world tells us who to be. We've been trained to let go of our childish ways.

Be quiet!

Sit still!

Don't talk to strangers!

Color within the lines!

Be careful!

It's just the way things are. Don't rock the boat!

I certainly remember those refrains being yelled at me time and time again by my parents, coaches, and teachers. And while they were well intentioned, in the process our natural buoyancy gets slowly squashed. Our inherent creativity gets coached away. Our playfulness and energy get disciplined right out of us.

Their exhortations diminish the senses required to effectively navigate the world in which we live. This affects the way we see our world, and how we show up in it.

Our senses are designed to help us process and understand the world. They inform what we see, hear, feel, taste, smell, and touch. When we lose access to them, we start to perceive a skewed, less vibrant, and distorted version of reality.

As we age, our senses diminish: vision blurs, hearing fades, taste dulls, our sense of smell declines. But we have other senses that we lose touch with as well. Senses that inform our opinions of ourselves, our connections with others, our perspectives on time, our ability to view life with wonder, and our ability to bravely step forward into it with nothing held back.

While it may be difficult to revive your physical senses, for some senses the damage isn't permanent. We can reawaken them. We can rediscover them. We can recalibrate them. And we can utilize them to get back to that state of awe.

Once rekindled, these senses have the power to transform our days and revolutionize our lives. They can improve our ability to innovate at work, connect authentically in relationships, and solve some of the very problems that plague the adult world today.

After interviewing thousands of business owners, thought leaders, and world changers, I've discovered that the very senses responsible for making them successful and effective today are the same traits that flourished most beautifully within all of us as children. These senses are the key to how they dream greatly, innovate wildly, achieve impossibly, connect authentically, and impact profoundly. Most important, it's how they live so fully.

And it's how you can do the same.

Get ready to relearn what you once knew to be true.

Prepare to celebrate the ordinary and achieve the impossible.

It's time to unleash inspiration, meaning, and joy by choosing to live In Awe of every experience, every opportunity, every day.

Wonder

Asking Questions to Achieve the Impossible

LISTEN CLOSE TO ME—

ANYTHING CAN HAPPEN, CHILD,

ANYTHING CAN BE.

Shel Silverstein

wonder:

(V) THE ABILITY TO QUESTION, GET CURIOUS,
EXPLORE WIDELY AND PURSUE DOGGEDLY
ANSWERS, SOLUTIONS, AND OPPORTUNITIES
LEADING TO INNOVATIVE THINKING
AND ENDLESS POSSIBILITIES

1

The Path of Possibility

The roar of the crowd seemed to envelop me.

I walked over to the grand piano and settled myself at the bench. Wiped the sweat from my forehead with my suit-jacket sleeve, placed my hands over the piano keys, and took a deep breath. Noticing my heart racing, I couldn't help but wonder: *How the heck did I get here?*

I was onstage at the MGM Grand in Las Vegas, sitting at a piano, surrounded by more than eighteen thousand people.

They were cheering. For me. A guy with no fingers who was hoping to inspire them to imagine what was possible in their lives by doing something seemingly impossible on his own: playing the piano.

I caught my breath, then spoke into the microphone with a laugh, warning the audience to lower their expectations for this musical interlude, and raised my damaged hands as the reason why.

With that, I took a deep breath and began to play.

The doorbell to our family home in St. Louis rang.

Mom, seated next to me at the kitchen table, went to answer the door.

With a few moments to myself, I looked up from my plate and glanced around. I was still getting used to all the changes in our home.

The sticky, worn, green linoleum that once covered our kitchen had been replaced and was now bright pink. The dark oak cabinets had been swapped for lighter, new ones; the orange countertop had been replaced with a fashionable shade of mauve. The mid-seventies fixtures had been exchanged for the newest fads of the late eighties. Reagan was in the White House, Springsteen was on the radio, and our kitchen was rocking.

Just nine years old, I sat in the kitchen of our renovated house trying to wrap my head around everything that had changed since the fire five months earlier.

It wasn't just our kitchen that was different.

Our garage had been reduced to ashes; every room in the house had been damaged by flame, smoke, or water. My five siblings and parents had been forced into temporary housing for four months as our home was rebuilt.

I spent those months in the hospital, fighting for my life.

We were dealing with change in every aspect of our lives.

But my own life had changed the most.

Thick white gauze bandages covered nearly every part of my body. I looked like the odd love child of the Pillsbury Doughboy and the Stay Puft Marshmallow Man. Don't get me wrong—both are unforgettable characters, but few of us aspire to be their offspring.

The majority of the bandages covered thick red scars where my skin had mostly healed. Some of those wrappings, though, masked open, painful sores that hadn't.

The wheelchair I sat in was an immense improvement over the months I'd spent tied down to a hospital bed, the practice at the time to minimize joint contractions as burned skin tried to fuse back together. Spending that much time motionless caused my muscles to atrophy. I struggled with basic mobility because scars had accumulated over my healing skin, rendering walking again a distant, improbable goal.

And then there were my hands. When I looked at where my fingers used to be, I saw gauze. The doctors had amputated my fingers on both hands down to the bottom knuckles.

I tried to avoid looking at my hands, because every time I did, I confronted a barrage of anxieties: *How will I ever throw a baseball again? How will I be able to go back to school? If I can't return to school, how will I ever get a job?* Most discouraging, even at the age of nine, was the thought: *No girl will ever want to hold my hand.*

I was staring down at my hands as Mom reentered the kitchen. A few steps behind her I saw the unmistakable silhouette of Mrs. Bartello.

As Mom approached, I looked at her in shock and asked, "What is *she* doing here?"

She was our piano teacher.

None of the O'Leary kids wanted to see her enter our house. Because her appearance meant that whatever we were doing—watching TV, playing, studying—would have to stop, as our piano lessons were about to begin.

Although none of my siblings were wild about piano lessons, I hated them the most. I didn't want to play the piano; I wanted to play baseball. It wasn't concert halls where I imagined my talents taking me, but baseball stadiums. It wasn't notes I wanted to hit, but fastballs.

I'd always dreamed of playing professionally for the St. Louis Cardinals. I just knew that one day I'd put on that uniform, take the field, and play for my beloved hometown team. Those were my dreams at age nine. Similar to the aspirations of other young children. We didn't yet know to be realistic with our goals.

Yet even a child knows when it's time to awaken to a grim reality. The fire had robbed me of that dream forever. I'd never hold a baseball. I'd never play for the Cardinals or wear the St. Louis uniform. Painful as that fact was, I took solace in one beneficial aspect of my injuries: at least I'd never have to take a piano lesson again. There is a silver lining to every cloud, people!

So why on earth was Mrs. Bartello here?

Mom approached my wheelchair, bent down, and released the

brakes. She reversed my wheelchair away from the kitchen table and pushed me down the hallway into our family room.

"Mom, where are you taking me?"

My friend, I want you to take note of how she responded. Maybe jot it down somewhere. I recommend that you use her tactic with a student, spouse, child, or someone with whom you are having a disagreement.

She didn't murmur a word.

Not a word.

Talk is cheap.

Instead, Mom humbly, bravely, lovingly pushed me away from the spot where I'd been stuck in the kitchen and moved me toward a new destination, a new perspective.

As she pushed me, I looked up and sought, one more time, an answer: "Mom?"

Silence.

She rolled me to the piano, relatched the brakes, and calmly told Mrs. Bartello she'd be in the kitchen if we needed anything. She then walked out of the room, stranding me alone with Mrs. Bartello.

This gentle piano teacher sat down and pulled the bench closer to me. She took a deep breath, put her arm around me, and told me how proud she was that I was finally home. She'd missed our lessons together, she said, and was excited for me to play the piano again. She added with a certainty that surprised me, "Okay. Let's do this."

Then, as if nothing had changed in my life in the five months since she'd last seen me, Mrs. Bartello pulled out the sheet music for a song I'd been learning for my mom. Back then, I had fingers but little desire to use them to play piano. That lack of desire remained and was a hurdle we'd have to leap over together. But, of course, now it was far from the only one.

Looking back, I am amazed that Mrs. Bartello, and my mother, had the audacity to think it was possible. How do you even begin to teach a young boy with no fingers to play the piano? Aren't fingers a prerequisite?

I sat in that wheelchair, in front of the piano, on a morphine drip, with my hands wrapped in thick gauze resembling a boxer's glove. And it gets worse.

My right arm had little muscle mass, making it almost impossible to lift; my left arm was strapped into an airplane splint at a 90-degree angle from my body.

I felt totally useless and utterly confused about what we could possibly do together.

But somehow, for some reason, Mrs. Bartello was undeterred.

She took out a pencil and a rubber band from her purse. She wrapped the rubber band around my right "glove," binding the pencil to the end of my bandages. With this single pencil protruding from my right hand, Mrs. Bartello instructed me to begin playing the notes on that sheet of paper.

What followed was the longest thirty minutes of my life.

As I listlessly hit the piano keys with the pencil, I remember distinctly thinking: *I hate my mom.*

I could not believe she was making me take piano lessons in the condition I was in. The only good that came out of it was that eventually the lesson ended. At least I'd never have to do that again, I thought.

Which was true. Until the following Tuesday, when the doorbell rang again. Mrs. Bartello came back . . . and came back the Tuesday after that.

For five freaking years of Tuesdays!

Gradually, painfully, begrudgingly, note by note, a bewildered boy with no fingers, with ostensibly no chance of returning to life as it once was, learned to play the piano. First with a single pencil bound to the bandage on his right hand. Then one bound to his left. As the wrappings were removed, I learned to play with the tips of my knuckles and by rolling my palm, creating makeshift chords with the parts of my hands that remained.

Looking back on those Tuesdays, I realize that Mrs. Bartello and my mom weren't simply teaching me the piano. They had no expectations that I'd perform at a recital or enter any competitions.

They were developing something more important than musical ability.

By releasing the brakes on my wheelchair and by pushing me toward a goal that seemed unattainable, by seeing potential and hope where any reasonable person would see only disability and despair, they delivered a message, without speaking a word, that I needed to hear and to heed.

John, this fire may have robbed you of your fingers. But it did not take your life! You will not act as if it has. You possess the power to do what today seems impossible. You will confront hurdles in your life. You will face difficulties. You will need to come up with innovative ways to overcome the challenges that lie ahead. Things will be different than we had planned. But in time, things will be better than you can even imagine.

That was a vital message that I needed to hear as a young boy, struggling with uncertainty and self-doubt, facing seemingly overwhelming physical limitations. It's one I need to hear from time to time even today.

And I'm convinced it's a message many of us would benefit from hearing.

Um, John, that has never happened to me, you point out. *I've never sat at a piano with morphine coursing through my veins and bandages covering my body, staring at nubs that once were hands, wondering how the heck I was going to play a single note, let alone an entire song.*

My friend, though the circumstances might look different, I believe that feeling of impossibility and being overwhelmed is something we've all faced at various times in our lives.

Maybe you were tasked with a new project at work but didn't have the skill set needed, plus your plate was full with your everyday responsibilities. As the work piled up, as the pressure mounted, you sat staring helplessly at the piano keys and felt that overwhelming urge to give up.

Or maybe you found out you were pregnant again, in the midst of a season where you barely had enough energy, time, and money to keep yourself and your family going, let alone give birth to and take care of another baby. At a time that should have been joy-filled, you found yourself staring at your life, wondering how on earth you were going to get by.

Or go ahead and scroll through the headlines today. How can you not feel overwhelmed with the sobering stories of war, famine, lay-offs, shootings, indiscriminate violence and prejudice that fill our news feeds, extract our joy, and leave us feeling hopeless, dismayed, depressed, as if there is nothing we can do to make anything better?

We *all* have moments in our lives when we feel like we are expected to play the piano without fingers! The question is, do you throw up your damaged hands and walk away from the piano, or do you find a new way to create your song, the one you were born to play?

Rather than shaking your head, giving up, and canceling the piano lesson, I invite you to reconnect with your sense of wonder that ignites the audacious belief that with enough creativity and determination, nothing is impossible.

I don't mean "wonder" in the sense of something that inspires amazement and admiration. No, this wonder is far from passive. By wonder, I mean something we *do*. I'm talking about our ability to be curious, to inquire, to probe, challenge, and even doubt.

Our sense of wonder makes us question the way we've been doing things and encourages us to ask, *Is there a better way?*

Our sense of wonder allows us to stop taking every answer for granted and start questioning what we've been told.

Our sense of wonder permits us to once again become innovators, inventors, artists, and scientists.

Our sense of wonder invites us to remember that we have the power, if we choose to harness and focus it, to change the world.

That kind of belief, that kind of certainty, that kind of wonder can truly change everything.

Shoot for the Moon

It was a swelteringly hot day in Houston, Texas. The date was September 12, 1962. President John F. Kennedy was speaking in front of an audience of forty thousand people at Rice University.

Although it was only twelve days into the month of September, it had already been an eventful month. A 7.1-magnitude earthquake in

Iran killed more than twelve thousand people. The entire world was on edge on the eve of what was to become known as the Cuban missile crisis. Global financial markets remained sluggish. The Supreme Court had just ordered the admission of the first African American student to the segregated University of Mississippi.

It was a time of turmoil and tension, frustration and fear. There were natural disasters, political protests, and cultural uprisings.

Sound familiar?

It was with this background that the president prepared to speak in Houston. John F. Kennedy knew what was in the hearts and on the minds of the American people. He understood they were feeling bewildered, nervous, lost, and unmoored. And he set before them that day a grand, compelling vision, a mighty goal.

A goal many thought impossible, if not outright lunacy.

It was a massive dream, one that would require all the best of America: collaboration, brains, innovation, and determination.

He set before us the goal of landing a man on the moon before the end of the decade.

In an unusually lengthy and poetic sentence, he reminded those listening of both the weight of the challenge and the solution to it.

> But if I were to say, my fellow citizens, that we shall send to the moon, 240,000 miles away from the control station in Houston, a giant rocket more than 300 feet tall, the length of this football field, made of new metal alloys, some of which have not yet been invented, capable of standing heat and stresses several times more than have ever been experienced, fitted together with a precision better than the finest watch, carrying all the equipment needed for propulsion, guidance, control, communications, food and survival, on an untried mission, to an unknown celestial body, and then return it safely to earth, re-entering the atmosphere at speeds of over 25,000 miles per hour, causing heat about half that of the temperature of the sun—almost as hot as it is here today—and do all this, and do it right, and do it first before this decade is out—then we must be bold.[1]

It was an unprecedented vision.

A daunting task.

An impossible dream.

And yet before the decade ended, just as Kennedy had promised, Americans heard astronaut Neil Armstrong, upon stepping on the moon's surface, announce, "That's one small step for man, one giant leap for mankind."

A couple of guys, strapped into a metal lunar module launched 240,000 miles away from earth, landed safely on the moon, bounced around a little while thanks to the lower gravity of the moon, planted a flag, grabbed some rocks, took some pictures, got back into their vessel and returned home safely. All with computing technology far inferior to that found in your old flip phone.

It seems impossible.

But they did it. When Kennedy urged America and Americans to be bold, he was saying that to accomplish this goal, we would have to throw out the rule book, put our boundless creativity, curiosity, and determination to the test, and keep at it relentlessly until we accomplished our goal.

We had to utilize our sense of wonder. The sense that doesn't allow us to give up in the face of failure. The sense that is always seeking new solutions. The sense that prods us to ask questions, get curious, and dig deep to find the way.

This is how we make big moves and enact true change. We put our minds together and invite our sense of wonder to push boundaries, reject limits, and go where no one has ever gone before.

Regrettably, our government leaders today speak less of bringing people together to create something bigger than themselves and more about protecting what we already possess. Our focus as individuals seems to be less about how much we can accomplish together and more about getting through the day. Far more effort is spent guarding what we have than expanding what, and who, we could become.

Why have we stopped thinking differently, and aiming for the moon?

It's because we've lost touch with our sense of wonder.

And it's time to get reacquainted.

When you reawaken your sense of wonder, you'll find yourself coming up with new ways of approaching old problems, reinvigorated by endless curiosity. You'll break out of ruts and find yourself traversing new terrain. Yes, you'll probably at times feel a bit uncomfortable. And that's as it should be.

Because the decision to shoot for the moon demands we chart new paths. When it comes to moonshot thinking, the "same old, same old" will not do. We've got to cover new territory, invent new technology, see with new eyes, and do things differently than we've done them before.

So how do we do it? How do we get back in touch with our sense of wonder?

By asking five deceptively simple questions.

These five questions were an essential part of your vocabulary as a child. They lead us to do more, be more, ask for more, and in doing so, innovate more. They elevate the relationships you have, the work you do, and the life you lead. They transform the way you view your past, celebrate your present, and create your future.

Doesn't that sound like a worthy adventure to undertake? Well, turn the page and learn the first question that reawakens the desire to find a new, different, better way forward.

2

Why?

SOMETIMES I'VE BELIEVED AS MANY AS SIX IMPOSSIBLE
THINGS BEFORE BREAKFAST!

Lewis Carroll, *Through the Looking-Glass*

Why do I have to brush my teeth?
Why do I need to use the bathroom?
Why is it bedtime?
Why can't boys have babies?
Why can't I sleep with my shoes on?
Those are but a partial list of the questions my children asked me—last night.

The list they asked yesterday was far more expansive. In fact, research has shown that four-year-olds ask up to three hundred questions per day![1]

If you have young children, work with them, or spend any time around them, sometimes it feels more like three hundred questions per minute. Although my kids are no longer four, I've got four of them. And they question everything.

While it often feels like their questions are fueled by the need to infuriate me, the reality is, they are simply supremely curious and deeply inquisitive about the way the world works.

Buried within those questions is the innate desire to understand the world.

In fact, famed astrophysicist Neil deGrasse Tyson believes children are our most natural scientists, leading the way with their curiosity and questions: "Kids are always turning over rocks or plucking petals off of flowers. They are always doing things that, by and large, are destructive. That's what exploration is. You take stuff apart whether or not you know how to put it back together."

Sounds good, right? I can handle a little exploration.

Until . . .

Your child pulls an egg out of the refrigerator. "And what's the first thing you do as a parent?" Tyson asks. You yell, *"Stop playing with the egg. It could break. Put it back."*

Yep, I've definitely done that a time or two.

Tyson's point? As he puts it, "Let the kid find out that when it drops, it breaks! This is a physics experiment. . . . We don't have enough parents who understand or know how to value the inquisitive nature of their own kids because they want to keep order in their household."[2]

We don't mean to do it. But as we try to rein in our children's impulse to understand and engage with the world around them, we inadvertently squelch their sense of wonder and inherent curiosity.

And we don't just do this to our children.

When was the last time you welcomed a well-timed "Why?" When was the last time you finished your strategy session, patient handoff, or team meeting, not with tactical next steps, but by encouraging constructive dissension, urging others to freely ask why?

With the goal of efficiency and maintaining hierarchical constructs, we shut down questions and dissenting opinions at work. At home. In our political discourse.

But asking why springs from a desire to understand the world and seek out its mysteries. Curiosity is a gift that we must reclaim if we are going to live In Awe. In fact, after I had spoken to a room of senior Microsoft leaders, one approached me afterward crediting their success not to knowing all the answers but to asking the right questions. If a $125 billion organization can celebrate asking questions, maybe we might benefit as well.

We may resent it when we are trying to get our kids to bed or keep our houses neat. But it turns out that asking why is essential to our survival. It is the key to understanding why things are as they are and questioning whether there is a different, better way.

When we stop asking why—as individuals, in our organizations, and as a society—we stop innovating, investigating different approaches, and instigating new ideas.

Here's an example. Watch any political commentary, tune into your favorite sports team's talk radio show, or check your social media feed. As adults, we seem to celebrate individuals with a firm, snarky, set-in-stone stance. With this tone as our soundtrack, many of us become quick to judge, immovable in our opinions, easily incited, and ready to retaliate against anyone who dares to disagree. Unfortunately, this negatively impacts our ability to come together and collaborate and prevents us from being open to new opinions, people, ideas, and ideals.

But we weren't always this way. We once were open and unafraid to question.

While watching a televised town hall designed to be a healthy, unifying place to discuss gun violence in the aftermath of yet another school shooting, I perked up my ears when I heard a student begin to speak. She was from Marjory Stoneman Douglas High School in Parkland, Florida, and had witnessed seventeen of her classmates die, while another seventeen were wounded.

Not even old enough to vote, still visibly shaken by the loss of her friends, this student filled her time not with statements or statistics but with questions: "Why can't we go to school without worrying about being shot? Why can't we collectively live in a society where gun violence doesn't claim lives by the dozens? Why can't we use the law to make things better for everyone? And why can't it start now?"

The room filled with applause as she finished speaking. The next panelist, who was described as an expert on gun violence and on the laws that govern our nation and states, sat with his arms crossed over his chest. As the room quieted, he smiled wryly and said, "I think you need to graduate high school, go to college, and get an actual education. Then we can discuss this."

Now, I'm not saying you should agree with the young student's views. In fact, you don't need to agree with anyone. But I think we can all agree that it's beneficial to stay open to new ways of solving old problems.

Why squash the vibrancy, agency, and hope that student exuded?

Why not embrace the willingness to investigate what we are doing wrong, and perhaps forge a better path forward?

While I'm confident few would be as insensitive as that panelist, I think many of us adorn ourselves with his brand of cynicism. We think someone whose beliefs and ideologies differ from ours must be wrong. So we shut down the conversation. And in crossing our arms against new ideas, we succumb to the status quo.

We squash our sense of wonder so far down it has no air to breathe.

How might our returning to the mindset of inquisitive students affect the manner in which we think, lead, solve, and connect? Rather than entering a conversation as smug, self-assured "experts," with answers to everything, how might showing up as passionate, compassionate, open-minded seekers influence the outcome not only of that conversation but of any conversation?

When the young people of Parkland banded together to create one of the largest protests ever held in this country, *Time* magazine commended their "ferocious optimism . . . There's a sense that anything can happen in this little corner of the teenage universe, because all kinds of things can."[3]

Ferocious optimism. That's a powerful phrase. And one I think we can all aspire to embody.

Ferocious optimism doesn't take no for an answer. Ferocious optimism requires that we look honestly at the world we inhabit, the businesses we lead, the teams we're on, and the lives we live, identifying not only things as they are, but imagining how they could be.

Ferocious optimism is the exquisite by-product of inviting *why* back into our lives.

Everything I Need to Know
I Forgot Since Kindergarten

While the panelist proposed additional education would help the young woman from Parkland find a way forward, research shows that the longer kids remain in school, the *fewer* questions they ask.[4] In fact, because many teachers want students to provide answers, not questions, perhaps the mindset we had when we first entered kindergarten is the one we need to return to.

Let me explain.

Did you know that most children about to enter kindergarten score at the "genius level" for divergent thinking?

Divergent thinking, though it sounds like a cool mash-up of a young-adult novel and a TED Talk by Bill Gates, is really just scientist-speak for thinking outside the box. Divergent thinking is the mindset that recognizes that there are multiple ways to solve a problem. It strives to come up with unusual solutions that are vastly different from the norm.

Divergent thinking is what happens when imagination, innovation, curiosity, and creativity converge.

And it is the root of all world-changing inventions.

The moonshot? It required divergent thinking. The Internet? The result of massive divergent thinking. The iPhone? Yeah, you guessed it.

Without people who are willing to push the boundaries of the status quo and strive for novel ideas, we would still be hunting and gathering for food, riding horses to visit neighbors, or sleeping in caves.

So how do we know that kindergarteners are so good at divergent thinking?

Professor George Land conducted a creativity study in children, using a test he had devised for NASA to help them select the most innovative engineers and scientists. It was a relatively simple test: He put people in a room with an average, everyday paper clip and asked them to come up with as many ways to use a paper clip as possible. Over time, Land observed sixteen hundred different children ranging in age from three to five years old.[5]

And he was astonished by the results. On average, each of these children imagined two hundred different uses for that simple metal contraption (and not all of them were "stick it in a socket to see what happens"). In fact, the very mindset that necessitates socket protectors when babies become mobile (and curious) toddlers liberated these young children to come up with all those ideas for how to use a paper clip.

Curiosity and creativity go hand in hand.

Which explains why a whopping 98 percent of those children who were tested scored at the "genius level" for divergent thinking.

So you're thinking, *Cool! We start out smart and we just get smarter. Right?*

Wrong.

Professor Land later did this study on adults. Do you know what percentage of adults scored at the genius level?

Two percent.

No, that isn't a typo. Two percent of adults scored at the genius level for divergent thinking. The typical adult came up with ten to fifteen ideas for how to use that paper clip.

Let's pause and let that sink in: Before entering kindergarten, before "learning" anything, we are creative geniuses. And then, over time, we lose our creativity, our ability to think differently, and our innovative, playful, and pioneering spirit.

Land was so intrigued by the initial findings of the experiment that he tested the same children again at age ten and at age fifteen to see how their creativity evolved over time.

By age ten, only 30 percent score at genius level.

By age fifteen, it's dropped to 12 percent.

Wow. That happened quickly.

So what happens as we mature that prevents us from thinking outside the box? What is it in our world, our culture, and our lives that leaches out our creativity?

And what can we do to stop the erosion of this essential, life-giving, world-changing power?

Let's lean into Adam Grant, an organizational psychologist at the University of Pennsylvania and author of the bestselling book *Originals*. Grant has an intriguing theory about what happens to us along the way: "Kids are inherently creative. If you talk to a five- or six-year-old, they have all sorts of interesting, unusual questions. And I think we either beat that out of them or they end up unlearning it at some point when they realize that the way you succeed, at least in Western society, is you follow the rules. You try and get good grades, you respect your elders, you go out of your way to fit in as opposed to stand out, and that's a great way to forget how to think differently."[6]

Let me repeat that. *Fitting in is a great way to forget how to think differently.*

If you think about it, our schools reward one type of kid: the rule follower and the good listener. As kids progress through school, they realize that asking questions doesn't get them gold stars. In fact, questions get them in trouble. So they stop asking. They start following. They stay quiet. They learn to answer the questions asked of them, not the other way around.

They begin to forget how to think differently.

This trend continues, by the way, in the vast majority of environments where we work, serve, and play.

When you stop asking why, you stop coming up with new ideas.

Because within the question *why* is the follow-up question that lies at the heart of all improvement, innovation, and inventions:

Why are things as they are . . . and is there a better way?

Imagine how this one simple question might challenge the status quo in your health, your spiritual journey, your personal finances, or your relationships.

What solutions might arise when you ask *why* with your team members, whether on new projects or as you review traditional practices?

Can you visualize how this could challenge and empower us in the way we view our businesses, our communities, our nation, our government, and our economy?

Why are things as they are . . . and is there a better way?

Why isn't for the faint of heart. It requires comfort with dissension and leads to potentially disruptive discussion in your personal and professional lives. Things may get a little messy along the way. You may break a few eggs. But that's okay. Get out some paper towels. Don't be afraid to shake things up or take things apart.

Why is the catalyst to innovative thinking, allowing us to pause, reassess, and seek a different, better way.

And there is one.

Always.

3

Says Who?

"I WAS JUST THINKING," SAID THE SPIDER, "THAT PEOPLE ARE VERY GULLIBLE."

"WHAT DOES GULLIBLE MEAN?"

"EASY TO FOOL," SAID CHARLOTTE.

"THAT'S A MERCY," SAID WILBUR.

E. B. White, *Charlotte's Web*

I fly quite a bit in my line of work. And my time on the plane is usually reserved for writing.

Unless I find myself seated next to one of my kids.

A few years ago a business trip provided me with an opportunity to bring my wife and kids to Australia. Patrick, who was five at the time, sat next to me and busied himself with studying a map of the United States. He was amazed that roadways connected the entire country. As cool as flying was, he somehow seemed even more in awe of the fact that we could drive to every state in our country.

Except for Hawaii.

So he declared that when he grew up he was going to start a company that would find a way to pave a route to Hawaii.

No matter how many reasons I gave for why it would never work, Patrick looked up at me and asked one question: "Says who, Dad?"

Finally I suggested that he map out on his napkin how he would build his bridge. Knowing I'd just bought some time, I went back to the writing. But not before looking over at Patrick, out the window at all that water and thinking: *Maybe there is a way to build a bridge to Hawaii!*

There was something about his insistent desire to question my "no," to push back against my desire to talk sense into him, that made me wonder: *When was the last time I said, "Says who?" Whom am I allowing to dictate whether I try something or not?*

Although we don't often stop to think about it, each of us is influenced by the opinions of those around us. From the media, to friends and family, to our own internal dialogue, these voices coalesce to inform what we believe is possible. And what we feel certain is impossible.

But frequently, those voices are just plain wrong.

A few weeks later, I was seated across from a young man who soon proved this very point.

A good friend of mine asked if I'd spend a little time visiting with his son. The young man had been in and out of various colleges, switched his major several times, and was finally a semester from finishing a business degree. As adulthood loomed, he seemed listless and uninspired, unwilling to apply for jobs or truly anticipate what might come next.

After making some small talk, I asked what he planned to do after graduating. Lowering his coffee mug, he shifted uncomfortably in his seat and said: "I don't know. I assumed that's why we were meeting."

Maybe his dad hadn't introduced me accurately. I wasn't a career coach. Sure, I helped people take steps on how to embark on their best life, but this kid had to give me something to work with!

Taking a different approach, I asked him what he wanted to do with his life, business degree and profession aside. "If you could do anything after graduation, and you knew you would not fail, what would you do?"

He looked away from me and out the window. A smile lit his face. And he spoke about his love for airplanes. In fact, for the first time since we sat down together, his voice came alive and seemed to sing with excitement.

He told me that for as long as he could remember he loved the idea of flying. He used to make model airplanes as a kid, he drew them in his free time and knew that someday he wanted to work around them.

He didn't care whether he was a pilot, a flight attendant, an aviation mechanic, or the guy who cleans the airplane lavatory; he just wanted to be around planes.

I listened intently and then asked the obvious question: "So what's holding you back from doing exactly that?"

His smile disappeared.

He looked out the window. Took a sip of coffee. Looked up at me. And responded: "I am too old."

"How old are you?"

"I'm twenty-four."

"Dude!" I responded. "I have ties that are older than you!"

But he shrugged off my comment. "Like I said, I'm too old. I've already put all this time into this degree. It's too late."

He was twenty-four years old. The vast majority of his life awaited him. And he thought he was too old to pursue a life doing what he loves.

So I asked the question Patrick had peppered me with a few weeks earlier.

Says who?

Who exactly is it that says a twenty-four-year-old is too old to make a career change?

Who says just because you start down one path in life you can't pivot, even wildly, and begin heading down another?

Who says we must accept what is, rather than dream and build what could be?

He was not too old. I knew this from firsthand experience.

I was seven years into a career as a real estate developer when I first spoke in front of a small group of Girl Scouts about being burned in a fire. I had no idea that that one speech would be the first step toward a new career path, and that my life would pivot so wildly at age twenty-seven. But if I had believed that it was too late, that I was too old, that my path was set in stone and led in only one direction . . . well, you certainly wouldn't be reading this book.

So I sent my friend's son on his way with that question, and prayed he would listen to a different voice and pursue a path that lit him up with excitement for his life.

My friend, whose voice, opinion, or "expertise" defines and limits your life?

What might happen if we had the guts to disagree with the voices that have held us back? What might happen if, when told we're too old or too young, too inexperienced or too insignificant, we boldly responded: Says who?

I've met countless individuals who have refused to let age or expectations limit their lives. Perhaps my favorite example is Marie Dorothy Buder.

At age fourteen, Marie heard a voice calling her into a vocational life as a religious sister. Though her parents had other plans for their daughter, by age twenty-three she formally entered a convent.

Sister Buder spent the next several decades serving the downtrodden in her community. She loved her work and felt totally committed to her life as a servant of God. But she sometimes felt plagued by an ill-defined anxiety. A good friend suggested that she try running. It might help to get outside and exercise her body each day.

Sister Buder didn't have any running shoes. In fact, she had never owned a pair. So she borrowed some from a fellow nun and went out for the first run of her life. She was forty-eight years old.

As she slowly put one foot in front of the other, at the pace of a gentle jog, she loved the way running made her feel. She relished the breeze on her face. She enjoyed the singing of the birds. She even loved the fatigue her muscles experienced as she made her way back home. So she made a commitment to go running the following day. And after that second run she was determined to go out again.

In the four decades that have followed, rare are the days when she *doesn't* lace up those shoes and go for a run.

But I tell you this not because she is a nun who occasionally runs in her free time. I tell you about Sister Buder because today she is eighty-seven years old and has run more than three hundred and fifty marathons. She is called the "Iron Nun" because she has also run several dozen Ironman races, an absurdly difficult test of physical endurance reserved only for the truly courageous and slightly delusional. It begins with a 2-mile swim followed by a 112-mile bike ride. Oh, and then you run a marathon, 26.2 miles, to top it off. World-class, well-trained athletes spend years preparing for this race. The vast majority of participants never cross the finish line.

Sister Buder is one of those indomitable athletes who has crossed the finish line. In fact, she has completed the race more than a dozen times, and at the spry age of eighty-two, became the oldest person to do so.

Seriously. I hope you didn't just spit out your coffee!

I know many forty-two-year-olds who get winded walking through the grocery store. Conventional wisdom, common sense, and well-meaning friends would argue that no one should be attempting an Ironman at age eighty-two. But Sister Buder dares to disagree.

I had the pleasure of taking her out to lunch to discuss why she keeps running. With a shimmer in her eyes and smile on her face, she told me that running brought her joy, and racing gave her confidence. The reason she still runs, though, was more about mission and recognizing that her simple willingness to show up at races encourages others to keep going in theirs.

As a young girl, she didn't listen when her family pleaded with her not to waste her life on a vocation. At forty-eight, she refused to listen to the voice saying it was too late to begin running. At eighty-two, she didn't heed the advice of the experts when they suggested she'd never finish the Ironman at that age. Nor does she listen now when others encourage her to slow down, to accept her age, to hang it up.

Not a chance. A very different voice guides her steps than guides many of ours. But that doesn't have to be the case.

So, who are you listening to that holds you back? Who in your work, family, or network keeps reminding you it can't be done? While we all need to listen to the voices of others along the journey, we ultimately need to be guided, inspired, and driven by the voice of truth. You have the capacity, the ability, and the power to disagree with their opinions. You have the authority to wonder: Says who? And you have the faculty to surge bravely forward with dreams of your own.

All right, you may not want to lace up a pair of running shoes to achieve those dreams, but know that the voice we choose to listen to influences the quality of the race we run. So ask yourself: Where in my life have I let limiting beliefs keep me from going after what I truly want? In a relationship? In my career? And where have I let what others deem impossible hold me back?

There will always be people trying to influence your direction or judge your actions. But just because the "experts" say it can't be done doesn't mean you have to listen.

Limitless

For generations, scientists claimed that to run a mile in under four minutes was physically impossible. The well-documented research of the day proved indisputably that the oxygen debt that would build up in the human body would be too great. The body would begin to shut down due to lack of oxygen, and the runner would be at risk of death.

A British medical student named Roger Bannister set out to prove them wrong.

Using his medical background, Bannister knew the key to breaking the four-minute mile was to manage his oxygen level throughout the race. That's what all the experts claimed was the challenge. To the critics and denigrators who considered it an impossible feat, Bannister replied: Says who?

He began to measure his oxygen consumption religiously during his training. He quickly learned that he used less oxygen when he ran consistent lap times than when he altered his pace. If he was going to break the record, he would need to run at the same speed for each of the four laps.

After careful documentation and months of training, on May 6, 1956, at a track meet at Oxford University, Bannister laced up his running shoes and did what had previously been declared impossible: He ran a mile in 3 minutes 59 seconds.

His feat instantly became front-page news around the world. The unbreakable record, the impossible barrier, had been broken. It was a breathtaking achievement.

Here's the most amazing aspect of his feat: His record in the mile run lasted just forty-six days before another runner ran the mile even more quickly.

Think about that: A goal that had been pursued for decades, regarded by experts as simply impossible, was finally achieved, only to be surpassed six weeks later. And it was broken three more times that same year. Today, the feat has been accomplished by thousands of runners, even high school students.

All thanks to one man, who was willing to say: Says who?

While Bannister displayed amazing discipline, training habits, and athletic prowess, the real lesson Bannister taught humanity that day was about not the body but the mind.

What we listen to, we believe.

Whose voice are you listening to . . . and who says they're right?

If the news as presented by the media is bringing you down, stop watching. If your friends and co-workers are too often naysayers, challenge them to change, or find new friends. And if the voice in your head is whispering negativity, it's high time to replace it with a new song.

What would happen if, when you are told you can't do things or you can't handle a certain task, you dared to disagree? To engage your sense of wonder and say: Says who?

Not like a petulant child, with disrespect for authority. But with a kind, curious, adventurous spirit, simply pushing back against or testing the limits.

Once we are no longer afraid to challenge the status quo, we'll start to see possibilities around every corner.

4

What Do You See?

ABOVE ALL, WATCH WITH GLITTERING EYES THE WORLD
AROUND YOU BECAUSE THE GREATEST SECRETS ARE ALWAYS
HIDDEN IN THE MOST UNLIKELY OF PLACES. THOSE WHO
DON'T BELIEVE IN MAGIC WILL NEVER FIND IT.

Roald Dahl, *The Minpins*

When I was ten, I heard some words that no child should ever have to hear.

My parents and I left our home a little before 4:00 A.M. We drove six hours, to another city, to visit a new hospital and meet with a new doctor. We were tired, a little apprehensive, and extremely excited. My parents and I were looking for hope.

After being released from the hospital months earlier, I'd continued to struggle with my inability to do much with my hands. Piano lessons aside, my fingers, or what was left of them, no longer had the ability to grasp things. After much research, my parents discovered two world-class surgeons capable of cutting into the palm of the hand, creating fingers from the webbing, and providing some dexterity for me.

We sat in front of the first doctor, eyes wide with hope and possibility. After he finished examining me, he quickly scanned my chart, looked my parents in the eye, and flippantly said: "If he was a horse, I'd shoot him."

My parents stared back at him in shock.

We couldn't get out of that hospital room fast enough. We barely spoke on the drive home. We were hurt, sad, and angry. Far from being the type of people who didn't see a reason for hope, we believed in miracles.

One of the reasons I beat the odds and survived my burns, despite all predictions to the contrary, was that we surrounded ourselves with the kind of people who saw hope and possibility. The doctor who had said he'd shoot me was the opposite.

He'll remain nameless in this book, but I'll never forget him. Or how he made me feel.

Two weeks later, we visited the second world-class surgeon. We waited for almost an hour in the most aptly named of spaces: the waiting room. When we eventually were led back, we waited a bit longer in one of the examining rooms.

While we sought a better outcome than last time, we were also aware that we might get more bad news.

When the door finally opened, a short, white-haired doctor breezed into the room singing, sat down, and opened up my file. His singing stopped as he clapped his hands together. He looked up with excitement and practically sang out the proclamation, "What is this? I get to see John O'Leary today? This little miracle boy I've heard about is coming to visit with me? What luck is this?"

He clapped his hands again, shut the file, stood up, and moved toward the door, singing again, as if to exit, before stopping in his tracks. He looked over at me, acting startled to see me seated on the examining table.

He walked over to me, took my right hand in both of his, looked into my eyes, and asked, "Are *you* John O'Leary?"

With a grin on my face, I nodded.

"Oh, I've been so looking forward to the honor of meeting you, and serving as your doctor."

This was Dr. Pappalardo. I looked at my parents with a smile. Maybe this was our guy.

After Dr. Pappalardo thoroughly reviewed my chart and my hands, Dad, bracing for more bad news, asked cautiously: "Well, what do you think, Doctor? What do you think of the prospects for John's hands?"

Dr. Pappalardo took both my hands tenderly in his own. He looked into my eyes, and then back at my dad, and said, "They are as beautiful as an Italian sunset!"

A spirit of hope infused that small room, as well as a little boy's heart. We knew this was our surgeon.

Dr. Pappalardo's joy extended beyond that first meeting. Every time he poured hydrogen peroxide on my hands after a surgery, he'd proclaim, "Pop the champagne!" as I watched it bubble and fizz upon making contact with my skin. Afterward it was time for an "ice cream party," as he'd carefully massage white cream on my hands before rewrapping them in their bandages.

Through four surgeries, this man's enthusiasm seeped into my soul. He allowed me to see the good in life and to celebrate each victory, however minor, as we fought for the best life possible.

One doctor saw a child without hope. He walked into the examining room with harsh "facts" and a projection of despair.

The other doctor saw reason to throw a party. He viewed me as valuable, my hands as beautiful, and my life as ripe with potential.

So what do you see when you look at others? Are you someone who is going to shoot the horse, or are you going to throw a champagne party?

The way we choose to view others impacts our interaction directly and dramatically. It influences how we feel about them, speak with them, and connect to them. It determines not only what happens in the moment, but also what transpires next.

There is power in choosing what you see. Consider beginning each of your conversations (in particular those with individuals you don't know or who may hold opinions you disagree with) by singing out: "You are as beautiful as an Italian sunset!"

Now, I don't encourage you to sing those words aloud, but what is sung in your heart will be reflected in your interactions. It will elevate the way you view others. And it just might inspire those you encounter to change the way they view themselves.

Change the Lens

It was a hot, sunny summer Saturday. I collapsed in the grass next to my little girl, Grace. She was six years old, tanned from weeks in the sun, and we'd just finished playing a game of baseball with her brothers in our backyard.

I had just closed my eyes when Grace asked me, "What do you see, Daddy?"

"What do you mean, baby?" I asked, my eyes still shut, basking in a moment of summer quiet.

"Up there," she said. Before I could respond, she told me: "I see a plane. Do you see it, Daddy?"

As I opened my eyes, I saw a blue sky, a few clouds, and a bright, brutally hot summer sun. No planes. So I looked over at her. She was shielding her blue eyes from the sun with one hand while pointing with the other.

She looked over at me, back up at the sky, and said again, "Do you see it now? It's a plane. What do you see?"

It was then I realized she wasn't talking about an actual plane, but the shape of the puffy clouds drifting by.

I laughed. Playing along, I said that I saw a unicorn. Grace nodded, then pointed out a cloud that looked like a face. We spent the next few minutes lost in our imaginings before getting up to rejoin her brothers.

It was the kind of simple, magical moment that happens all the time to us in childhood. But by the time we've reached adulthood, too many of us have forgotten to look up into the clouds and to recognize that what we see in those clouds above is entirely up to us.

Several years ago I was getting ready for work when my son Jack walked into the bathroom as I was shaving. For a while he pretended he, too, was getting rid of the "stubble" on his cheeks. But then I noticed he'd stopped his pretending and was gently touching the scars that cover my torso.

They are deep red scars, with ridges and lumps that traverse my stomach. When I look at myself in the mirror, even today I often avoid looking at my stomach. It's just too painful. It reminds me of all I went through, and would sometimes rather forget.

But on that day, my son, then about five years old, traced with his little finger the scars that are evidence of what I've gone through in my life. And he said something that surprised me.

"Daddy?" he said.

"Yeah, bud?" I replied.

"Your tummy is red, it's bumpy, and it's ridgy. . . ." He paused, but continued tracing his finger along the scars. I was preparing to let him know that Dad might be different, but that it was okay. But before I could explain away what I imagined to be his fear and anxiety, he said:

"And I love it!"

I was stunned. My eyes welled with tears.

That wasn't what I was expecting. But my boy, I am happy to say, was like Dr. Pappalardo. He could see beauty, hope, and joy, even, in those scars. He saw an Italian sunset. He saw that those scars might make me different, but don't define me, and he loved them.

What if we could each be like Jack? Stop reading. Get up, find a mirror, look into it, and answer this question: What do you see?

It's okay. Take your time. I'm not going anywhere.

Go ahead. Look at your wrinkles. Your gray hair, or lack of hair. Your eyes. Your bumpy or ski-jump nose. Look closely. What do you see?

Do you see signs of aging, signs that life is headed downhill? Do you feel frustrated that you'll never measure up? Do you see what you could have been, but aren't?

Or do you see signs of wisdom? Do you see how the experiences of yesterday aged you, yes, but also grounded you in humility, gratitude, and a deep sense of interconnectivity with the human race? Do you see evidence of the scars not as something to be ashamed of, but as something to trace, to celebrate, to even love?

What we see matters.

But as my kids are continuously teaching me, we have the freedom to *choose* what we see.

What do you see? And how can changing your perspective change your life?

It is easy, as we age, to grow into skepticism, to scoff at those who still dance, and give in to cynicism. H. L. Mencken summed it up beautifully when he wrote that a cynic is a man who, when he smells flowers, looks around for a coffin. That is how much our perspective can affect how we see the world.

But what if, instead, we could be like Dr. Pappalardo? What if we could discover champagne parties in the bubbling of hydrogen peroxide and ice cream when we apply burn ointment? What if, in seeing burned, scarred, damaged hands, we could imagine Italian sunsets?

It's a choice we all have. We choose how we will perceive the realities that surround us.

For me, those two perceptions were the difference between life and death.

Dr. Pappalardo performed four radical surgeries that gave a boy with no usable fingers the ability to hold a pen.

The ability to type this sentence.

To brush my teeth.

To hold my wife's hand.

And to live my life.

Dr. Pappalardo's sense of wonder was engaged, and his ability to get curious and imagine the possibilities gave me life.

When we see only impossibility, we shut down the opportunities before us, not only for ourselves but for those around us.

I'm not suggesting you sugarcoat the difficulties of life or sweep painful realities under the rug. But the path of possibility recognizes that no matter how hard life gets, there is power in how you respond. So start digging. Go on a treasure hunt. What new things are you going to discover as you look around your community and your business, as you examine your relationships and your life, and dare to see them differently?

Because if you only want to see the dark side, the disappointment, you'll most assuredly find it everywhere you look. You'll feel validated.

But if you seek champagne parties and Italian sunsets, you'll discover them wherever you look, too.

Some people see *impossible* as a limit.

Others see it as an opportunity.

Choose wisely.

5

What If?

OH, THE THINKS YOU CAN THINK UP IF ONLY YOU TRY!

Dr. Seuss, *Oh, the Thinks You Can Think!*

Have you ever met someone who turned out to be nothing like you expected?

That's exactly what happened when I first met my good friend Mick Ebeling.

We met at a conference where we were both invited to speak. I was taken aback by this tall, lanky guy wearing a flat-brimmed baseball cap, looking much more like a guy about to hit the skate park than a corporate event.

But when he began his presentation, I was transfixed.

Mick's been committed to making the world a better place since he was a child. He was constantly challenged by his parents to leave things better than he found them. That value remained with him as he launched a successful career working at an animation and design studio.

When a friend invited him to a fundraiser at an art gallery for a beloved graffiti artist, Tempt, Mick was eager to attend. Tempt had been diagnosed with amyotrophic lateral sclerosis (ALS) at age thirty-four and was now paralyzed. Mick was captivated by the stunning artwork he saw on the walls, and later sat down with the artist's family to offer a financial contribution. He thought he would meet Tempt's family, they would have a short conversation, and he'd move on with his life.

But that conversation sparked an idea that changed the course of Mick's life.

Tempt's brother told Mick that the thing he found most frustrating about Tempt's situation was his inability to talk. "I just want to be able to talk to my brother again, you know? I just want to be able to communicate with him."

Mick had never thought about the fact that someone whose body is completely immobilized isn't able to talk, let alone write. The only part of Tempt's body that he could move was his eyes. He "communicated" by having someone hold up a sheet of paper with the alphabet on it and blinking when their finger crossed the letter that he wanted to use to spell out his intended word.

When Mick came to this part of his story, if he'd seen me in the crowd, he would have observed me wiping away tears.

I knew all too well how Tempt felt, and how frustrated that artist must have been. When I was in the hospital as a nine-year-old, for the first six weeks after the fire, I was intubated, which meant I had a breathing tube inserted through my mouth. I could not speak. The only way I could communicate with my family and the doctors after going through one of the scariest and most traumatic events of my life was by using a piece of paper with the alphabet on it. In my case, I would click my tongue when they got to the letter I wanted. It was excruciatingly slow and frustrating, and often led to my just being silent.

I only had to endure this type of communication for six weeks. Tempt had been living this way for seven years.

Onstage, Mick went on to share what he'd done at that moment, sitting across from Tempt's brother. Instead of shrugging helplessly and sympathizing with Tempt's brother, he couldn't help but think: *Man, that's not right*.

While he did not know how to cure Tempt's paralysis, he knew there was something he could do about his ability to communicate.

Mick told Tempt's brother that he would find his brother a device so that he could "speak" via computer. While Mick didn't have the exact technological skills to build one himself, he knew such devices existed. The family mentioned that the astrophysicist Stephen Hawking, who also had ALS, had used one, but unless you are in the upper echelons of society, it is incredibly hard to get access. The insurance companies just won't shoulder the expense.

Well, Mick beat down the doors of the insurance companies and eventually got Tempt the device he needed. His family was incredibly grateful.

In the process of his research, Mick had been connecting with people who were developing life-changing technology that could be applicable for those with Tempt's condition. One such group was Graffiti Labs. Mick was telling his wife about their work over dinner one night. Graffiti Labs had been creating pop-up graffiti installations across the world, beaming a laser from afar to create light graffiti on historic sites like the Washington Monument. Because they "painted" with light, it wasn't permanent and didn't deface the monument. Mick loved that they were disrupters, rule breakers who were also incredibly creative.

Mick's wife was impressed. "That sounds really cool. What if we could use lasers to help Tempt paint again?"

In that moment, Mick realized his wife had made a brilliant suggestion.

Mick soon invited a ragtag group of hackers, innovators, and engineers to move into his house and work together until they figured out how to make this seemingly impossible feat happen. By the end of two weeks of trial and error, endless experimentation, and countless prototypes, the team had created the Eyewriter.

Using a combination of eye-tracking software and high-tech drawing software, they had built a pair of wired-up eyeglasses that allows the person wearing them to move his eyes where he wants to "draw" on the computer. And it allowed Tempt to paint again.

It would later be named one of the top fifty inventions of 2010 by *Time* magazine.

The first time Tempt was able to use the laser pointer to create again, he said, "It feels like taking a breath after holding my breath underwater for five minutes."

Soon they combined their Eyewriter with the technology used by Graffiti Labs to allow Tempt's creations to be beamed via laser to the side of a building just outside Tempt's hospital. As he lay in his hospital bed inside, the team was outside, watching—in the darkness and cold, with their hearts in their throats—as Tempt's unique artistic signature began to appear out of nowhere, on the side of the building. The crowd erupted in cheers as they saw the creativity of an artist who had been silenced for seven long years. A man they had all come to love.

It was indescribable. Breathtaking. Awe-inspiring. Watching *impossible* morph into *possible*.

And that was just the beginning.

Shortly afterward, Mick founded Not Impossible Labs. He and his team identify problems that seem absurd, that make them say: *That isn't right. That has to change.* And they commit to figuring out how to solve those problems. They have created prosthetic arms with 3-D printers, so that people in war-torn countries can have access to these life-changing tools. They have helped the deaf community experience music. All of their creations are open-source and free to the public. Their motto is "Help one, help many." They don't want their creations to just help one person. They want their technology to spread widely and be available to all.

I love Mick. I love his heart, his creativity, his impact. And perhaps most of all, I love his unwillingness to accept the impossible.

"Everything that surrounds us today at one point did not exist," he said to me when I had the chance to connect with him again, when he was a guest on my *Live Inspired Podcast*. "It was impossible. So the inverse is true: Everything that is impossible today is on the trajectory of becoming possible. It might not be at this moment, in this lifetime, but it's gonna happen."[1]

That belief that there is an answer is what keeps Mick, and every other inspired leader, going. They see a need and they care enough to do something about it. They dig deep, looking widely for solutions, experimenting until they get it right. They aren't comfortable with or willing to just accept the status quo, but search expansively to find an answer.

Their sense of wonder, fully engaged, allows them to ask "What if?"

And if the solution they come to doesn't work, rather than wave a white flag of surrender, they go back to the drawing board, back to the team, back to the problem, and ask again, "Well, what if?"

My friend, we've got to stop being boxed in by the way things have always been done.

The problem is, our brains don't always work that way.

Heat It Up

Remember the study that showed that kindergarteners were better at the paper clip test than adults? There is a physiological reason for that: Kids' brains are wired completely differently from adult brains.

Our brains are designed to become efficient with age. They draw from our previous experiences and make educated guesses about what will happen next. It's called predictive coding. When our brains continually guess the same outcomes over and over, it alters our neural pathways. They get edited down from a million different potential pathways to a few, well-traveled boulevards.

By the time we are adults, our brains have been trained to quickly determine the answers to questions. What's 2 + 2? The answer is 4! What's the capital of Missouri? It's Jefferson City! This seems to serve us well in the test-taking culture of our educational system, and even in the get-things-done-quickly-and-efficiently corporate world.

But if we are to question the way things have been done, if we are to cultivate our sense of wonder and "what if," if we are going to get back to experimentation, then we've got to prevent our brains from only pursuing quick answers. We have to be willing to waste some time, come up with ridiculous ideas, and pursue paths that no one has gone down before.

This is the path of innovation.

Unfortunately, here is what typically goes on in our adult brains when we're confronted with a problem: In the pursuit of efficiency, our adult brains conduct what the field of artificial intelligence calls "low-temperature searches." Low-temperature searches don't take very long or require much effort; they tend to seek an answer that worked for a problem that we solved previously. Those well-traveled boulevards, right?

But children? They conduct what AI calls "high-temperature searches." These searches are more wide-ranging and seek out *new* answers, rather than ones that have worked in the past. They also take longer and expend more energy. Oh, and they are more likely to get it wrong! They are the winding alleyways that may or may not turn out to be a dead end.

But they also return solutions that are original, innovative, sometimes radically wrong, and oftentimes fundamentally transformative.

High-temperature searches seek and find endless possibilities. (Or two hundred different ideas for those paper clips.)

Alison Gopnik, a professor of psychology and an internationally recognized leader in the field of learning and development in children, has done fascinating research on the way children's brains work and how they are so different from our own: "Early in life we are sensitive to more possibilities, while later in life we just focus on the possibilities that are most likely to be important and relevant to us."[2]

What she is saying is that when we are kids we are in tune with the world of infinite possibilities. We are conscious of all the options. Our eyes are wide open, our imaginations wild, our opportunities unlimited.

As we age, though, our brain changes and our experiences inform what we believe we can do next. Our eyes narrow, our imagination becomes tamed, our options dwindle.

In fact, Gopnik created a test in her lab and found that when presented with a challenge that required unconventional thinking or an unlikely hypothesis, four-year-olds solved the problem much quicker than adults because adults were doing low-temperature searches, looking for the most common solutions, while children were still engaged in high-temperature searches. Their capacity for asking "What if?" remains fully engaged and rewards them with endless possibilities. Thomas Edison, one of the greatest inventors in the history of the world who, as such, lived by the question "What if?" is reported to have said: "When you have exhausted all possibilities, remember this: You haven't."

Mick Ebeling lives by this belief. He told me, "Sometimes people with the degrees behind their names solve the problems, and sometimes they *are* the problem because their experience and degrees and diplomas . . . make them think they know best. . . . Sometimes what you need is beautiful, limitless naïveté."[3]

Man, I love that.

Beautiful, limitless naïveté.

The willingness to admit that you don't know what you don't know. That you are ready to go on an adventure to uncover answers, that not knowing doesn't scare you, but is actually an invitation to go on a journey—the journey of "What if?"—and figure it out.

"What if?" is the key to discovering new options. It opens doors. It is the question of hypothesis, of experimentation, of scientific breakthroughs, of self-discovery.

While we cannot fight against our brain's pruning of our neural pathways, we can recognize when our brains are reaching for the easy answer and work to reawaken our ability to do a high-temperature search. We can be like Mick Ebeling and commit to solving a problem, then work through the many different ways we could figure it out. This is what organizations do when they encourage a brainstorming session. They are saying: *Let's think outside the box. Even if something seems stupid or unreasonable, let's reserve judgment and see what we can come up with*. It is an attempt to invite the question "What if?" back into our lives.

Is there something that you are facing today that feels impossible?

A relationship that appears to have run its course?

A job that feels like a dead end?

A child struggling with direction, addiction, or acceptance?

A life that seems mundane, unfulfilled, or lacking in meaning?

What might happen if you used the power of "What if?" and applied it to those impossible problems? If you, like my friend Mick, were determined to do what you could to solve them, no matter how long it took, or how many failed attempts?

> **What if when you saw the impossible, you had the beautiful, limitless naïveté to seek a different way?**

Children don't have a problem admitting what they don't know. It's when we become experts, when we think we know the answers, that we are at greatest risk of not only losing sight of all we don't know, but also of all that could still be.

What if, as Muhammad Ali said, the term "impossible" is just a word thrown around by people who find it easier to live in the world they've been given, rather than to explore the power they have to change it?

It was impossible for a kid to survive burns on 100 percent of his body.

It was impossible to launch a space capsule to the moon.

It was impossible to run a four-minute mile.

It was impossible for Tempt to communicate.

Until all of these things were made possible.

In fact, everything that is possible today was once considered impossible.

Everything.

As you read this, what feels impossible in your life? What relationship seems too far gone, professional hurdle feels too high, social wrongs look impossible to right, or personal dreams appear simply too outlandish to achieve?

How might inviting wonder back into your life allow you to discover just how far you could go?

What if you started now?

6

Why Not?

THERE IS NO LIVING THING THAT IS NOT AFRAID WHEN IT FACES DANGER. THE TRUE COURAGE IS IN FACING DANGER WHEN YOU ARE AFRAID, AND THAT KIND OF COURAGE YOU HAVE IN PLENTY.

L. Frank Baum, *The Wonderful Wizard of Oz*

I had flown to Las Vegas the evening before and had just completed the sound check and run through the slides for my talk. I had a few minutes to myself before the doors opened and the event began.

Glancing to my right, I saw a grand piano on a secondary stage for a performance later that afternoon.

I walked over to it and looked around to see if anyone was watching.

I sat down and stared at those beautiful white ivories. I peered around one more time, and then, with no one telling me to "step away from the piano, sir," I began to play. Better to ask for forgiveness than permission, right?

My wife, Beth, and I had recently seen Coldplay perform at a similarly sized arena, so I punched out a few chords from one of our favorite Coldplay songs, "The Scientist." I imagined the rush that Chris Martin must feel every time he's onstage and is surrounded by fans singing along to his music. As I got to the refrain, the words "Nobody said it was easy" were echoing in my ears, as someone behind me spoke up, "I didn't know you played the piano."

I stopped playing, shut the lid, and sheepishly turned toward the voice. "I don't!"

My face flushed at being caught in a daydream.

One of the leaders who had planned the meeting that was about to take place approached me with a smile on her face.

"Well, I was standing right here and it certainly sounds like you know what you're doing." After a pause, she asked, "Would you play for our group later today?"

As you know, I grew up being forced to take piano. For years those Tuesday afternoon lessons were the worst part of my week!

In time, though, what was mandatory shifted into something I came to love. Although I don't have fingers (and Chris Martin isn't peering over his shoulder in fear that I am coming for his job), I love to play today. Beth and I have an old upright piano in our house. I play it on occasion to relax after a long day or to spark creativity before beginning a new project. Some evenings we'll jam on songs like "Heart and Soul" as a family. I'll play one hand and one of my kids will play the other hand.

But this wasn't my family room. It was a stage in the amphitheater of the MGM Grand. This wasn't an intimate family room filled with my kids, but an arena that would soon be filled with thousands of strangers.

It just wasn't something I was ready to do. It was above my pay grade! So I responded the only way a sane individual would: "I don't think that's a good idea."

"John, I think it's a great idea . . . and it would mean a lot to me and our consultants."

I wanted to refuse. I wanted to say no. This seemed like a ridiculous request, and the thought of it terrified me.

But then I thought about my mom. I thought about her taking a child sitting at a kitchen table and releasing the brakes on his wheelchair. Pushing him forward toward something that seemed impossible.

Why was I putting on the brakes now?

So I began to ask myself: *Why not?*

Why not say yes? Why not show a little courage and vulnerability, and do something that scared the heck out of me?

Why not do more than just tell the consultants who would be filling the seats how we can all survive and thrive through adversity? Why not show them? Why not prove to them that though things may seem impossible, when you have the right team by your side, they will help push you forward, challenge the status quo, and show you just how high you can aim, how far you can reach?

It was the perfect way to share this lesson with this audience.

Now, don't get me wrong. Brakes exist for a very important reason. They keep you safe. They keep you from rolling into oncoming traffic. They prevent the pull of gravity from catapulting you down a steep hill.

But the brakes on your vehicle, and on your life, aren't meant to be on all the time. If you always keep the brakes of your wheelchair latched, you won't have a *wheel*chair anymore, you'll just have a . . . chair.

How often do you have the brakes on in your life?

In my experience, when we get stuck doing things the same way we've always done them, we have the brakes on.

When we accept that the status quo is as good as it's gonna get; when we listen to the voices that say it can't be done, including our own; when we see only discord and difficulty, and decide not to even try; when we believe that things are impossible; it means the brakes are holding us back.

I may not be sitting next to you at your kitchen table, but I'm here to release those brakes and push you forward into what might come next in your life—if you have the courage and creativity to start doing things differently. To remember the endless possibility you felt as a child, and get back in touch with that whimsical sense of wonder.

My mother did more than release my brakes that day. She taught me to see, just over the horizon, what I could not yet see for myself. To fight, regardless of adversity. To stride bravely forward, no matter the unlikelihood of success.

And to not let what looks impossible stop me from envisioning what could still be mine.

So as I finished my talk that afternoon, I walked over to that piano.

My heart pounded in my chest. I thought at that moment of my mom. I imagined how she would feel if she knew that her little John was about to play the piano in front of eighteen thousand people. All because of her love, and dedication, and endless belief in me.

And I played the song that always brought tears to her eyes when I played it for her: "Amazing Grace."

As the notes of that familiar song reverberated in that enormous theater, I realized the answer to the question I had been asking myself: How did I get here?

By embracing the challenges of my life rather than being limited by them, and letting them *launch* me.

By staying deeply in touch with the power of possibility, instilled in me by my mother and that dreaded, turned beautiful, compassionate piano teacher.

By asking questions, being filled with wonder, and believing nothing was impossible.

It's how I got here.

And it's how you'll get where you most want to go, too.

Sense #1: Wonder

Stay stuck in the way things have always been done?
Or

Invoke the transformational power of
asking old questions, open to new answers?

My friend, it's time to take off the brakes.
To return to the stance where you questioned everything.
There are new possibilities that await.
New solutions beckoning.
New paths begging to be taken.
If you dare to push, to prod, to get uncomfortable,
and to question.

Why are things as they are . . . and is there a better way?
Whose voice are you listening to . . .
and who says that person is right?
What do you see . . . and how might changing
your perspective change your life?
What if when you saw the impossible . . .
you had the limitless naïveté to seek a different way?
And why not release the brakes, so that you
can enjoy the ride of your life?

Not merely questions, but invitations to do life differently.
I know it's possible.
And now so do you.

Expectancy

Returning to the Powerful State of First-Time Living

"WHEN YOU WAKE UP IN THE MORNING, POOH,"
SAID PIGLET AT LAST, "WHAT'S THE FIRST THING YOU SAY TO YOURSELF?"

"WHAT'S FOR BREAKFAST?" SAID POOH.
"WHAT DO YOU SAY, PIGLET?"

"I SAY, I WONDER WHAT'S GOING TO HAPPEN
EXCITING TODAY?" SAID PIGLET.

POOH NODDED THOUGHTFULLY.

"IT'S THE SAME THING," HE SAID.

A. A. Milne, *Winnie the Pooh*

expectancy:

(N) TO LOOK TOWARD THE FUTURE WITH THE DEEP
CONVICTION THAT ADVENTURE AWAITS AND
AMAZING THINGS ARE POSSIBLE

7

Bring Your Glove

LET THE WILD RUMPUS START!

Maurice Sendak, *Where the Wild Things Are*

One in a thousand.

That's your mathematical chance of catching a ball if you attend a Major League Baseball game.

Those aren't great odds. If you really want to take home a baseball, let me give you some advice: Bring a few extra bucks and buy one from the souvenir shop.

Perhaps that's why I felt a little cynical when I saw my son Patrick carting his baseball glove as we loaded up the car. Every summer I take an overnight trip with each of my children. My kids review my speaking schedule, pick the location they want to visit, research the city, and make plans for what we'll do when we get there. I act as if the trip is for them, but really, it's a gift for me.

During the summer of 2017, Patrick chose Kansas City. It was an easy call: One of his favorite cousins lived there, there was a Legoland downtown, and the St. Louis Cardinals were scheduled to play the Royals the evening of our arrival.

When I saw him exit the house with his baseball glove, I knew what he was thinking. "Bud," I said with a smile, "let's leave the glove at home. The best-case scenario is you'll get hot with it on during the game, and the worst case is you'll leave it behind in the stands."

Not persuaded by my logic, Patrick shook his head and said confidently: "Dad, I'm gonna need it."

Well, in the eighth inning that evening, his words proved prophetic.

A ball careened off the field, bounced high over the stands, and spun directly toward us. As I ducked to avoid impact, I heard the crisp sound of ball smacking leather.

I looked over at my son. The ball had plopped perfectly into his waiting glove, and Patrick's face was lit up with the sheer joy of a dream coming true.

Man, I thought, *what a lucky kid.* I've been to hundreds of games over my lifetime and have never returned home with a baseball.

I gave him a hug and celebrated with him. *What a lucky kid. One in a thousand. Hope he savors this moment . . . because it will never happen again.*

Ralph Waldo Emerson wrote: "Shallow men believe in luck, believe in circumstances. . . . Strong men believe in cause and effect."

I didn't realize how shallow I was.

The following summer, as we prepared for our annual trip, our destination was Pittsburgh, hundreds of miles away. As soon as Patrick got in the car, I saw it.

Already on his left hand, even though we had eight hours of windshield time in front of us. His glove.

I bit my tongue and allowed him to have his fun. He wore that glove for the eight-hour drive, and each time I saw it, I smiled at his unbridled optimism. Little did he know our seats were high up in the right-field stands and about as far from home plate as you can get!

We arrived just as the game was starting. We watched several innings from our seats in the outfield before taking a lap around the stunning ballpark. We got some snacks, took some pictures, and returned to our seats a few innings later.

Just as we sat down, the Pirates' third baseman crushed a ball toward us. The ball soared just over our heads, bounced off several sets of hands, and was corralled by a bear of a man seated three rows behind us and about ten seats over.

Wow, that was pretty close, I thought, my heart racing as fireworks exploded in the sky and the Pirates fans celebrated.

As things settled down, we took our seats. Out of the corner of my eye I saw the man who had just caught the ball standing at the end of our row. He was looking at us and pointing at Patrick, who stood out from the locals in his bright red Cardinals baseball cap.

"Hey, kid!" he yelled. "If you can catch this, it's yours. I want you to have something to remember this game by besides your team losing!"

He then underhanded the ball toward us. Patrick reached high and brought the ball down in his mitt.

I looked over at Patrick, his face aglow. And now, in his glove, against overwhelming odds, another freaking baseball.

He was now, unequivocally, the luckiest kid I'd ever met.

Shallow people believe in luck and in circumstances. Strong people believe in cause and effect.

The Expectation of Adventure

Today I am convinced it wasn't luck that brought those balls Patrick's way.

Sure, a bit of good fortune enters into the equation.

But you'll never catch a ball if you aren't in the stadium.

You won't see the ball if you aren't actively watching the game.

And you can't grab it easily unless you bring your glove.

Then why don't adults bring their gloves to the game?

Well, in addition to the fact that a big, bulky glove may not go with our outfit, we know the odds. We don't want to look like fools, hoping for a miracle. Seriously, when was the last time you saw adults walking into a stadium with their baseball gloves on? It doesn't happen. And if it did, what would you think about them? Be honest!

And yet, have you seen the transformation that takes place when adults see a ball coming their way? For a moment they turn back into little kids. They widen their eyes, jump to their feet, spill their drinks, drop their hot dogs, raise their hands high, all for the extraordinary chance . . . the life-changing opportunity . . . to catch a used baseball!

The anticipation rouses them from the complacency shrouding their day, and awakens the child within. They turn from cynics into believers in the span of a few seconds.

I'm not saying that we should walk around expecting to win the lottery every day. (In fact, I encourage you *not* to play the lottery!) But there is something powerful about moving through life, through work, through relationships, through each day, not readying ourselves for disappointment, but expecting adventure.

There is something life-changing that happens when we return to that audacious, unguarded, optimistic mindset of a child.

The stadiums of life today are mostly packed with bystanders, arms crossed, gloves long ago stored away. Rather than expecting adventure, we aim for realism. We try to protect ourselves from experiencing false hope.

Sure, we once believed life was a great adventure waiting to unfold. But those days are long gone. We've been beaten and battered along the road of life. We've endured bumps and bruises, sometimes scars that last. We think those wounds have wised us up.

In fact, they can blind us to what is really going on around us, and within us.

Here's some data about how bad things appear.

According to recent polls, only 28 percent of Americans are optimistic that the country is headed in the right direction.[1] This isn't just a result of a new administration or changing economic situations. Since 2012, U.S. polls reveal citizens to be more pessimistic than optimistic about the future. More than half of all Americans polled feel that the United States is at the lowest point they can remember in history.[2]

Adventure? What adventure? We're just trying to survive!

Jeffrey Sachs, a professor of sociology at Columbia University, calls the plight we're in a social crisis. "When confidence in government is low, when perceptions of corruption are high, inequality is high and health conditions are worsening . . . that is not conducive to good feelings."[3]

Why write a book about living In Awe in the midst of these dire statistics?

Because I want each of us to recognize how bad things are. No, not due to the realities around us, but to the mindsets within us.

You see, those polls that I quoted don't reflect the facts. They reflect our *perceptions*. They measure our fear and our cynicism and our doubt. Our expectations about where we think society is headed.

Don't get me wrong. The challenges we face as a society are significant. Injustice, inequality, and poverty. Nagging tensions between governments, mounting concerns with the environment.

We face adversity individually, too. Relationships are complicated. Health is fleeting. Job markets shift. Friends disappoint. With nearly 50 million of us struggling with mental health, the path forward can at times feel incredibly lonely and sometimes downright hopeless.

Life is hard. By no means am I trying to sugarcoat the hardships we face in life. But the rise of cynicism, negativity, and fear-based thinking must give way to radically different mindsets if we are going to address this social crisis.

Consider this: What if it wasn't luck but Patrick's attitude of expectant anticipation that allowed his dream to come true (twice)? What if, in choosing an attitude that keeps cynicism at bay and rejects the odds, we actually increase the likelihood of our desires becoming reality?

I know you're thinking that this kind of mindset is unrealistic, and perhaps even downright stupid. Pollyannaish. Impractical.

Which is why I'm going to prove to you how a shift in perspective is, in fact, incredibly practical, more than reasonable, and how the life-altering benefits are scientifically proven.

You won't need luck, just a willingness to grab your glove, uncross those arms, forget the odds, and see what happens when you recalibrate your sense of expectancy.

8

First-Time Living

THEN LET'S LOOK ON THE BRIGHT SIDE: WE'RE HAVING AN
ADVENTURE . . . AND MOST PEOPLE LIVE AND DIE WITHOUT
BEING AS LUCKY AS WE ARE.

William Goldman, *The Princess Bride*

Everything is awesome!
Everything is cool when you're part of a team.
Everything is awesome!
When you're living out a dream.

So goes one of the most annoying, and most listened-to, songs I know.

The song was written for *The Lego Movie* and was nominated for Best Original Song at the 87th Academy Awards. If you aren't familiar with it, I invite you to google it right now, and listen.

When you do, that song will be stuck in your head for days.

You're welcome.

Because of a DVD that my kids refused to allow me to eject for several months, that song seemed to play more than a million times on our television set alone.

Each time the upbeat, obnoxious music would begin, I'd roll my eyes, thinking, *Not again!*

But my kids—and I think all kids—didn't know the song was written tongue in cheek. They think the words are accurate and worth singing.

In its neurotic, hyped-up glory, that song encompasses the way children approach life. They genuinely think it is awesome.

Have you ever seen a kid at a shopping mall excitedly riding an escalator? They stand in stunned amazement at the marvel of a moving staircase. *What? My feet aren't moving. I'm going up. It's like a metal magic carpet ride. This is awesome! Can we ride it again?*

It's not just escalators, either. Ever see kids search for worms on a rainy day? Or sat near one the first time they flew on an airplane? Or witnessed their first jump off the diving board?

Yep. All awesome.

Kids, because they haven't done things before, are endlessly excited about even the most ordinary of things. They approach situations with eyes wide open, ready to be thrilled, ready for awesomeness.

Because their brains are still developing and determining how to categorize objects, situations, and experiences, children walk forward into new experiences not knowing what to expect. This can be dangerous (it's why they require parental supervision), but it is also an incredible way to experience the sheer joy of life.

It is first-time living.

Adults have long ago lost touch with this experience. We've seen it all before. We know how things work. Escalators simply take us to the next floor. Worms are gross. Airplanes are dirty, frequently delayed, and always cramped. Diving boards are for kids.

But when our minds and hearts were young, we literally hadn't been there or done that yet. Everything—truly *everything,* from a ride on a bus to a bug on the ground—was worthy of exclamation because it was something that we had never done before, never seen before, never experienced before.

Children are connected to their sense of expectancy, and that sense is tuned to expect excitement and adventure. They see exciting things everywhere they look, and expect there is more of that in the future.

But as we age this sense gets recalibrated. Instead of expecting awesome, we let the disappointments of the past shadow our expectations for the future. Instead of one big exciting adventure, life becomes a struggle to endure the downhill slope.

Denying the Decline

The other night, my wife and I watched a movie in which Billy Crystal plays a character who is facing middle age, and all that comes with it.

In one scene, Billy attends career day at his kid's school. He has been working in the same job for years, selling advertisements on the radio. As he tries to describe his job to the kids in the room, one student asks with great excitement, "Wait, are you a DJ on the radio?"

"No," Billy responds. "I sell the ads that air on the radio."

Another asks eagerly, "Do you write the jingles on the ads?"

"Nope," he says, getting frustrated. "I just sell the ads themselves."

His consternation mounts as he dejectedly looks down and the kids seem to recognize just how unfulfilling and boring his job, and his life, are.

So in a monotone, despairing voice, he offers this sage advice:

Value this time in your life, kids, because this is the time in your life when you still have your choices. It goes by so fast. When you're a teenager, you think you can do anything, and you do. Your twenties are a blur. Thirties, you raise your family, you make a little money, and you think to yourself, *What happened to my twenties?* Forties, you grow a little potbelly, you grow another chin. The music starts to get too loud, one of your old girlfriends from high school becomes a grandmother. Fifties, you have a minor surgery (you'll call it a procedure, but it's a surgery). Sixties, you'll have a major surgery, the music is still loud, but it doesn't matter because you can't hear it anyway. Seventies, you and the wife retire to Fort Lauderdale. You start eating dinner at two o'clock in the afternoon, you have lunch around ten, breakfast the night before, spend most of your time wandering around malls looking for the ultimate soft yogurt and muttering, "How come the kids don't call? How come the kids don't call?" The eighties, you'll have a major stroke, and you end up babbling with some Jamaican nurse who your wife can't stand, but who you call mama. Any questions?[1]

It is a hilarious scene, performed with the kind of faintly annoyed tone that Billy Crystal is able to pull off beautifully.

Sure, his diatribe is a bit of an exaggeration. But can't we all relate to the sense of drudgery that he describes?

Look around your office, your cubicle, your home, your life . . . doesn't it sometimes feel as if the adventure is over? Like Billy, we know where we're headed. And it ain't always that good.

It doesn't have to be that way.

Regardless of the monotony of your days or the struggles you face, I'm going to show you what happens when we relearn what a child does naturally. I'm going to remind you of the gift of first-time living. And I know of no better example to share the impact of this mindset than my friend Pat Hyndman.

Pat retired more than three decades ago. While many of us associate retirement with lazy mornings, afternoons on the golf course, and evenings playing bridge, Pat took a different path. He embarked on a second career, one that was just as fulfilling as his first.

I had the chance to meet Pat when I was invited to speak at the monthly gathering of executives that Pat coached. Several of his friends had prepared me for the fact that Pat's health was failing after almost a century of living and a stage four cancer diagnosis that resulted in several rounds of chemo.

But when I walked into the room to see a man of clearly advanced years presenting to the group, I wasn't expecting to encounter such vitality and passion from a man who that day was turning ninety-eight.

When he saw me, Pat stopped speaking midsentence, put his pad of paper down, and said in a loud, welcoming voice, "Everyone, our guest John O'Leary has arrived from St. Louis. Let's welcome him!" He walked over, looked me in the eyes with a big smile, shook my hand firmly, and thanked me for making the trip.

During my three-hour session with the group, while every executive took notes and was engaged in the presentation, no one was as dialed in as Pat. I could feel him soaking up every word I said, and could see him writing vigorously in his notebook.

After the session, we celebrated Pat's ninety-eighth birthday.

As we sang "Happy Birthday," he looked as joyful as a kid, wearing a playful smile and using his hands to spiritedly conduct our singing.

What I remember best about that day is that after our serenade, Pat went around the room and spoke to each person in attendance. He thanked all twenty-five business owners by name, shared something he respected about them, and specifically why he was grateful they were a part of his life.

Although I'd met him just four hours earlier, he included me in the celebration, thanking me for waking up early, catching the flight from St. Louis, leaving behind my wife and kids, and joining the group today.

He made each person feel as if the entire party was for them, rather than him.

At the end of the evening, as Pat was putting on his coat to go home for the night, I asked what fueled him each day. What allowed him to keep going to work with such energy and enthusiasm, keep fighting through chemo, keep showing up for life?

"You know, John," he said with a smile, "life is a gift. And I treasure each day I'm given. I've discovered that a person begins aging only when they stop learning and stop loving."

"Plus," he added, "I made a promise to my wife, Bonnie, seventy-three years ago to stay by her side. I intend to keep that promise."

He winked at me, gave me a hug, and then headed out the door, saying, "I better get home soon or she'll think I'm running around on her!"

Less than two months after that conversation, Pat went home for the final time. But not before keeping his promise to Bonnie, and being by her side when she passed away three weeks before him.

For nearly a century, Pat showed how we could live our lives with our sense of expectancy still fully engaged. No, he didn't look forward expecting pain and struggle. He knew that life is a gift, that every person matters, and that each day is packed with surprises.

Surprises only appreciated by those who choose to open their eyes wide enough to see them.

My friend, we have two very different teachers standing in front of us sharing two vastly different messages.

One is a character in a movie, age forty-five or so. He's in radio, has a decent job and a good life. He has his health, his family, and a large portion of his life in front of him. And he stands before the classroom sharing nothing but despair, reminding the kids not to blink, because life slopes downhill from here.

The other teacher is ninety-eight. He has stage four cancer, two months of difficult life ahead of him, has lost much along the journey, and deals with constant aches that rack his body. And he stands before the classroom reminding us not to blink, to expect nothing but joy, because life is a magnificent gift not to be missed.

Now, here's the point: We get to choose which teacher shapes our lives.

We get to decide which person we want to grow into.

We get to determine what kind of life we want to lead and what type of legacy we want to leave.

What if we could get back to a place where everything was awesome?

What if we could enter each situation with eyes that expect not routine, but adventure?

What if you looked at your spouse or partner today the way you did when you first met, wouldn't it revitalize your relationship?

What if you walked into your job with the anticipation you felt on your first day, wouldn't it change the way you worked?

What if you walked into your house and looked at your children with the awe that was present when they were first placed into your arms in the hospital, wouldn't you squeeze them a little tighter and make sure to sit down and converse about the day?

To get back to first-time living, we've got to get out of the rut of *been there, done that.* We've got to wake up to the gifts that are all around us, and have been from the start.

The fact that each one of us is here—it's nothing short of a miracle.

Perhaps it's time we start acting like it.

9

Stop Acting Ordinary

THE MAD HATTER: HAVE I GONE MAD?
ALICE: I BELIEVE SO. YOU'RE ENTIRELY BONKERS. BUT I'LL
TELL YOU A SECRET. ALL THE BEST PEOPLE ARE.

Alice in Wonderland, **directed by Tim Burton**

Have you ever done something you realize later was a big mistake? Yeah, that spring-break tattoo qualifies.

So do those words spoken out of anger to someone you love.

Yup, that weekend in Vegas, that decision to try a spray tan, that idea to save money by cutting your own hair, and that regrettable choice to wear capri pants all count.

And yes, in full disclosure, the above are but some of the mistakes I've made in my life! While I'm not proud of them, they are a few examples that are relatively safe to own up to in a book my wife, kids, parents, and dear friends might read!

I'm confident you've got your list, too.

If you read my first book, *On Fire,* you know that one of my greatest mistakes was following the example of some kids in my neighborhood as they played with gasoline and fire. As a nine-year-old boy, I couldn't wait to try to make fire dance myself.

That curiosity led me to sneak into our garage one Saturday morning, when Mom and Dad were out of the house. It guided me toward a five-gallon container of gasoline. Holding a piece of cardboard that

I had set on fire in my left hand, I tried to pick up the container of gasoline with my right. I wanted to pour a little bit on the flame to see it come to life.

Before the liquid came out, the fumes inhaled that flame into the metal can and the resulting explosion catapulted me twenty feet to the far side of the garage. It lit me on fire, and the entire garage was in flames as well.

My mistake changed everything. For me. For my family. For my future.

I was burned on 100 percent of my body. Eighty-seven percent of my burns were categorized as third-degree burns, the most severe and most deadly.

Doctors calculate the mortality rate for burn patients by taking the percentage of the body burned and adding the age of the patient. So, doing the math, take 100 percent of the body burned, add the age of nine, and you have a 109 percent likelihood of death.

I had no chance. It was hopeless.

So how am I still here, sharing this second book?

Well, you can read *On Fire* to learn exactly how it played out, but let me give you the CliffsNotes here. My seventeen-year-old brother and two of my sisters, just eleven and eight, responded to the explosion, acted with undaunted courage, put out the flames that engulfed me, and called 911.

I was fortunate to be placed in the care of exceptional first responders and healthcare providers. They viewed their work not as a job but as a calling. They ignored the statistics, striving instead to provide me every chance to survive.

My community stepped forward during the five months I ultimately spent in the hospital and over the years of recovery that followed. During an incredibly difficult time, we were strengthened by friends who came to visit and the kindness of strangers. Encouraging letters poured in from around the country and around the world. We believe God utilized those serving in my care and worked through even the most arduous experiences to deliver a miracle.

But the morning I was burned, we didn't know what was going to happen. Everything seemed lost. Our house was decimated. My body was devastated. The fire had burned through my skin, through my fatty tissue, even through my muscle in some areas. My heart raced and breathing was difficult. I was in intense pain.

My life seemed over.

Into this situation, into the emergency room, strode my mother. She saw how grim it was. She saw that my clothes and skin had completely burned off of my body. She knew how close I was to death. It was an indescribably terrible sight, yet Mom bravely walked right over, smoothed back my bangs, and told me she loved me.

Her presence, her voice, filled me with emotions. Since arriving at the hospital I'd wondered what would happen to me. The nurses and doctors were bustling around me, but no one was talking to me. So I responded to her love with a question.

"Mom, am I going to die?"

Without hesitating, she took my right hand gently in hers, and she said the words that would forever change my life: "Do you want to die, John? The choice is yours."

I didn't waver in my answer. "I don't want to die, Mom. I will not die. I want to live!"

Mom nodded. Then she gave me a challenge.

"If you want to live, you're going to have to fight like you've never fought before. You're going to have to take the hand of God and walk the journey with him. John, it won't be easy, but Dad and I will be with you. You can do this, but you must fight."

I nodded back at her, tears streaming down my face.

Before she entered into that room, I was scared, felt alone, and expected to die.

After she spoke, I was absolutely certain I was going to live.

I never wavered in that belief again. There was an uncommon, almost supernatural sense of peace that descended on the room that day, as she ushered in hope and awakened my belief that I could survive. I was going to live, get out, go home, and in time be even better because of this tragedy.

People often ask me: *How many times did you think you were going to die, when you were in the hospital as a little guy?*

The answer?

Not once, after the conversation with Mom.

I didn't know what procedures lay ahead. I didn't know the grueling pain that would be my constant companion. I didn't know how long my recovery would take. I didn't know what words like "tracheotomy" or "debridement" or "amputation" even meant—or that I'd experience them in the months ahead. But I knew with absolute certainty I would live.

That belief, that hope, that expectation was everything to me, a child trying to recover, heal, live.

It is a critical factor in why I am alive.

And as unlikely as it may be for me to still be here, it's just as unlikely that any of us are.

What Are the Odds?

After surviving the fire, after beating those dire odds, I knew that my life was a priceless gift. I stopped taking it for granted. I still don't. But have you ever contemplated the gift that is *your* life?

While driving through the stunningly beautiful countryside of Ireland, I had some time to reflect on how miraculous it is that any of us are here.

I was behind the wheel of a full-size van, packed with my family and loaded with luggage, navigating through the exceptionally narrow and curvy roads of Ireland. There were surprising periods of silence when the six of us quietly sat in awe, looking at the beautiful vistas outside our windows.

Silence doesn't last long with four kids in the family. My oldest son, Jack, broke the reverie when he asked how his mom and I decided where to attend college. Beth told him that she'd almost gone to a different school, in a different city, to become a nurse. But at the last minute she'd chosen the occupational therapy program at St. Louis University.

I told him about a few other schools I had considered, how I narrowed my choice down to just two, why I almost went to college in the South, and how, late in my senior year of high school, I pivoted, stayed close to home and attended St. Louis University.

Beth looked back at the kids and added, "You should be glad we changed our minds. Because if we hadn't, we never would have met." Then playfully she added, "And if we hadn't met, none of you would be here!"

As we continued our drive through the Irish countryside, I thought about the mighty strike of fortune that led to a family of six staring out the windows of a rental van. I soon realized the course of our lives ran much deeper than just our college selection.

Had Beth rushed a different sorority, or had I joined a different fraternity, or had one of us stayed home to study on a chilly January night in 1998, we wouldn't have met.

If my brother in the fraternity hadn't invited his friend Beth, or introduced us at the beginning of the night, if I hadn't indulged in a little liquid courage and asked her onto the dance floor, if she hadn't been bold enough to take my hand, or if we hadn't exchanged phone numbers at night's end, we wouldn't be traveling this road together.

If I hadn't stuck with our friendship (even though I wanted more) for three years, during which Beth finally began to see me as something more than her good friend John O'Leary, we wouldn't have finally had that dinner when she announced that she could see us being more than friends.

That dinner spiraled into three years of dating, sixteen years of marriage . . . and four kids in the back seat of a van maneuvering over the back roads of Ireland.

I marveled at the miracle that was our life together.

But what about your life?

Have you ever stopped to think about how you got here?

Dr. Ali Binazir, who calls himself "The Happiness Engineer," decided to do the math. To figure out the probability of *you* being born. The odds of one sperm (from the 500 million your father produced in his lifetime) combining with one egg (from the 200,000 your mother possessed) into the perfect union of your individual life.

The answer?

One in 400 trillion.[1]

Yep. Those are the odds.

To put those odds in proper perspective, the odds of winning the virtually impossible-to-win Powerball are 1 in 292 million. Meaning we're almost two thousand times more likely to win Powerball than to exist. Better go out and buy your tickets!

The prospect of any of us being here is incredibly unlikely. So you can choose to consider your life a lucky accident. A cosmic fluke. Chance.

Or . . .

(You knew that was coming, didn't you?)

Or we can look at those odds and realize our life is one of the most stunning gifts, a priceless treasure, a mighty blessing that is truly unfathomable.

Would you say you are acting and leading and loving and living like it?

Are you going to let your life pass by without truly enjoying the adventure?

You, like me, are here, against overwhelming odds. Let's not take it for granted.

Religious scholar Huston Smith said:

The opposite of the sense of the sacred is not serenity or sobriety. It is drabness; taken-for-grantedness. Lack of interest. The humdrum and prosaic. The deadly sin of acedia.

All other attributes of a realized being must be relativized against this one absolute: an acute sense of the astonishing mystery of everything.[2]

An acute sense.

Of the astonishing mystery.

Of everything.

That's awesome.

Children haven't lost touch with the mystery. They don't act ordinary, don't think life is ordinary, and certainly don't expect tomorrow to be ordinary.

Those who live In Awe can't wait to see what's around the corner, and expect wondrous things.

They see the future as filled with limitless possibilities. They embrace the astonishing mystery of everything.

And so can you.

10

Light It Up

HAPPINESS CAN BE FOUND EVEN IN THE DARKEST OF TIMES IF
ONE ONLY REMEMBERS TO TURN ON THE LIGHT.

Harry Potter and the Prisoner of Azkaban,
directed by Alfonso Cuarón

The sun was setting. The ocean breeze was gently blowing. The waves were breaking.

Henry was lying on a towel, hands clasped behind his head. After a long day of jumping in the waves, building sandcastles, and playing hard, he was finally slowing down and just taking in the changing colors of the evening sky.

I lay next to him, putting my hands behind my head to copy his posture. Together, side by side, we looked out at the stunning sunset.

After more than a minute, which in kid years is close to an hour, I looked over at him, and said, "Buddy, isn't it great to be alive?"

Henry looked back at me, swept his blond bangs away from his eyes, and responded, "I don't know, Dad. I've never been dead."

I laughed and turned back to the sky. He had a point.

But his comment stunned me.

I'd never considered that death wasn't something to avoid at all costs. We're taught to assume that death is the final frontier—something to dread and to put off as long as we possibly can. Even those who believe in an afterlife would rather stay put here on earth as long as possible with what is familiar, what we know.

And yet Henry had no negative expectations about death. For all he knew, it was the best party ever! He was reserving judgment. Sure, it was great to be alive. But death? Heaven? Heck, it might be even better than lying on a beach watching a sunset.

Oh, to have that much unbridled optimism and hope again.

Hope is in short supply in the adult world. Too many of us are mired in despair, despondency, and gloom. That's fertile ground for the opposite of hope: learned helplessness.

University of Pennsylvania psychologist Martin Seligman first coined this term as a result of his pioneering research. Learned helplessness is the state that we find ourselves in when we have been conditioned to expect that there is nothing we can do to change our circumstances. He first studied the phenomenon in dogs and rats. But he found it occurred in humans as well. Instead of resisting negative circumstances after repeated exposure to hardship, some people embrace a passive resignation to what is happening.

They will not even try to extricate themselves from a difficult situation because their past has taught them that nothing they do will help. When confronted with pain, suffering, and struggle, they don't try to avoid it because they believe their actions don't make a difference. Rather than fighting forward, or trying to change things, they just give up.

Unsurprisingly, learned helplessness is connected to higher rates of depression. Because when you no longer believe your actions matter, you feel like a perennial victim of circumstances, doomed to a life that is less than you desire. And you truly believe that there is nothing you can do.

My friend, guess what?

There is *always* something you can do.

The very best example of pivoting away from learned helplessness and toward possibility is the life story of a man named Andre. People call him "the Ambassador for Hope." Here's why.

Andre didn't know his father growing up. His mother worked a number of jobs, so when she was home, she was too tired to really engage with him.

The one light in his life was music. Andre loved to sing. When he was introduced to the trumpet in fifth grade, Andre fell in love. He could not get enough of practicing, playing, and performing. But one day after he started sixth grade, the other kids began making fun of his trumpet case. It may seem insignificant, but Andre longed to fit in. So he put away his trumpet. For good.

That dream was extinguished.

Andre found a sense of belonging through joining a gang. Soon he was selling drugs on the street. The next few years, he was in and out of juvenile detention for selling drugs, robbery, and assault.

When he turned eighteen, the actions that used to send him to juvie for a few months landed him in jail. The crimes he committed led to a prison sentence of eighteen to twenty-five years.

While Andre knew what it was like to be tough out on the streets, being sent to a maximum-security prison at age eighteen required a whole new level of toughness. If he didn't establish his place in the prison pecking order, he would be beaten and abused. So he became the violent one among the inmates.

Andre was so violent, so angry, so difficult to handle that he was moved to nine different state prisons over the years.

He was convicted of instigating a prison riot. He was convicted of attempted murder. Twice. These actions extended his prison sentence to one hundred years.

After the second conviction for attempted murder, he was sent to solitary confinement for two and a half years. He had just turned twenty-four years old, and was going to spend the rest of his life in prison.

Andre lay in the dimness of his small cell and contemplated the darkness of his life.

He was alone.

Locked up.

Cut off.

Hopeless.

But without the distraction of trying to look tough in front of others, Andre had time to reflect. Unless he changed the way he was acting, he would spend the rest of his life behind bars. And he didn't want to die in jail.

Andre continued to replay all the wrongs done to him over the years in his head. But in solitude, he got tired of that recording. So he dug back into his memories. He reviewed them, searching for a new song: the words of people who had once believed in him, people who had reached out a hand and had promised encouragement and hope. At the time, he'd been too wrapped up in his own pain to listen.

But then he remembered a third-grade teacher telling him he was a good person.

He recalled the music teacher saying he had a gift.

And a sixth-grade math teacher describing him as a fine young man.

An English teacher and a guidance counselor in high school encouraging him and seeing promise in his life even though he'd already made so many mistakes.

For the first time in more than a decade, he felt the glimmer of hope. If those people had seen something in him, maybe he wasn't too far gone. In the seclusion of that jail cell, Andre imagined getting out of prison, envisioned becoming a contributing member of society, and even pictured himself graduating from Harvard. Ambitious dreams for a guy who never graduated from high school.

Once out of solitary, he spent the next eight years transforming who he was into who he knew he could be. He taught himself to read. He earned his GED. He walked into a counselor's office and acknowledged that he had an anger management problem.

He met with a rabbi, who taught him the power of forgiveness. "I'd been taught how to make a knife out of a chair, how to not eat for three days, but no one ever taught me how to say I'm sorry."[1]

He met with two nuns he credits with not only igniting his faith but sparking his love for others, his love of learning, and his love of life. They taught him about redemption, and assured him that it remained possible for him.

The violent young man, angry at the world, was transforming into a forgiving sojourner, committed to ensuring that his future would be radically different from his past. While he was the one in metamorphosis, others were noticing the changes.

And at age thirty-two, Andre Norman, once sentenced to spend the rest of his life in prison, was released.

How do I know this story? Because Andre Norman is my dear friend.

The last time we connected we got in a fight, but it was a fight over who would pick up the lunch bill. Today he is a law-abiding citizen. He travels the world sharing his story. He's a devoted father, a published author, and an adjunct professor at a college you may have heard of: Harvard.

How does someone go from facing a hundred-year prison sentence and solitary confinement for attempted murder to teaching at Harvard? How did Andre pivot so drastically from a painful past to a bright future?

In a word: hope.

Hope is the fuel that powers us forward, no matter where life has us today.

Hope is the sacred light that allows a cancer patient to endure yet another round of radiation, chemotherapy, or surgery and the burdensome uncertainty of whether all the suffering and pain will be worth it.

Hope is the glimmer of possibility that encourages those between jobs to send out another résumé, to go to another coffee meeting, or to join another networking group.

Hope is what empowers every recovering addict, every achiever, every leader who's ever risked, attempted, failed, and fallen to stand back up, dust themselves off, and step forward again.

Hope just might be the most important renewable asset available to each of us in our lives.

The How of Hope

So how do you move from learned helplessness toward a life filled with hope? "Whether you are sitting in a boardroom or a jail cell doesn't matter," says Andre. "What matters is the moment you realize: *I don't want to live this life anymore.* The question is, are you going to find the courage to change?"[2]

Dr. C. R. Snyder, who studied hope for years and wrote six books on the subject, came up with Hope Theory. He believes hope is composed of three simple things:

1. *Goals.* You've got to have a dream.
2. *Pathways thinking.* You've got to realize there are a number of ways to pursue that dream, and to be ready and willing to navigate the twisting terrain.
3. *Agentic thinking.* Last, but certainly not least, you've got to accept that you have the power, the agency, to navigate through the obstacles that will inevitably get in your way.

Hope doesn't ignore the difficulties you'll face. It just doesn't let you give up in the face of them. Hope doesn't overlook that things get tough. It just doesn't permit the struggle to dissolve the dream.

In fact, according to Snyder's research, hopeful people can tolerate pain almost twice as long as those lacking hope.[3]

Hope sustained Andre through the years of study and therapy he needed to change who he was. It was hope that inspired his many appeals to the parole board. That allowed Andre to keep pushing, fighting, and growing as a person, believing that there was a way out of the jail he had built for himself.

Hope is fuel.

Christopher Reeve, who was the first actor to portray Superman on film, and was paralyzed from the neck down following an accident many years later, famously said: "Once you choose hope, anything is possible."

At the center of hope is the concept of self-determination: the belief that your actions can influence your future. In fact, it is the very opposite of learned helplessness. Agentic thinking declares that what I do matters. I own my life and my actions. Although I can't change what's happened in the past, I have the power to make things better.

Researchers at Indiana University discovered that hope was in fact a better indicator of success for incoming law students in their first semester of law school than their LSAT score.[4]

And if that doesn't impress you about the power of hope, try this: Dr. Stephen Stern, professor of psychiatry at University of Texas Health Science Center, performed a longitudinal study on hopefulness on elderly Americans between the ages of sixty-four and seventy-nine. Those who scored low on hopefulness were twice as likely to die during the follow-up period than those who reported strong feelings of hope.[5]

So, are you ready to get on the hope bandwagon?

The light and fuel of hope are necessary for a life lived In Awe.

We all have a choice. We can surrender to what is.

Or we can celebrate what might be.

Because the door to your cell is open. The guards have gone home. You are free to walk out.

But you've got to get up, move forward, and determine that where you are going next is better than where you've been.

Because our expectations determine not only the life we live today, but the one we're preparing for tomorrow.

11

Great Expectations

THE MOMENT YOU DOUBT WHETHER YOU CAN FLY, YOU CEASE FOREVER TO BE ABLE TO DO IT.

J. M. Barrie, *The Little White Bird*

When I was a child in the hospital, nighttime was my least favorite time of the day.

Partially because visiting hours would end and my parents would be forced to leave. But also because of the medicine that I had to take each night before bed.

When the body is working to heal burns, one of the side effects is intense, overwhelming itching as the damaged skin regenerates. Each night, the nurses administered a drug to help alleviate the itching. The only problem was, it made me sick.

The first time they added it to the cocktail of drugs flowing through my IV, I felt incredibly nauseous and threw up all over the bed.

The next night, as they gave me the medicine, I could feel my stomach already rumbling. And sure enough, I got sick.

The same thing happened the following night—and for the next seventeen nights. No one liked giving me the medicine. I was already suffering so much; did they really need to make me feel even worse?

One evening, a kind nurse took pity on me. She said she wanted to give me one night without getting sick. She wasn't going to give me the medicine.

I thanked her and enjoyed a night free from vomit.

Unbeknownst to me, the nurse had pulled my mom aside as her shift was coming to an end. She told my mom that she had in fact given me the medicine intravenously; she just didn't tell me.

That nurse knew that it wasn't the medicine alone that was making me sick. It was also my expectation that the medicine was going to make me sick. It was my anticipation of the nausea that brought about the nausea.

The mind is powerful. What you expect is often what you get.

This isn't just my experience, either. For decades researchers have struggled with this well-known and unexplained phenomenon during drug trials. To test the efficacy of the treatment in question, one group of participants would receive the proposed medication being tested, while another group would receive a sugar pill, called a placebo. Neither group knew which pill they were ingesting.

The researchers of course hoped that the group taking the drug would show signs of improvement.

But what shocked the medical establishment was how often the group that took the sugar pill *also* showed signs of improvement. Despite the fact that the only thing in their pills was sugar, because they *thought* they were taking medication that could heal them, their body responded as if they *had*.

Their thoughts—their brains—literally instigated the healing.

Now known as the placebo effect, this science-defying phenomenon has been studied for years. In one stunning experiment on people suffering from knee pain and stiffness, one group of patients had arthroscopic repair of their knees and finally began to experience less knee pain and become more active again.[1]

But here's the crazy thing: The group who unknowingly *didn't* receive the procedure, who had minor incisions made in their knee but no debridement of the cartilage, also reported less pain, and within months were back to playing basketball.

The placebo effect is real, and it is powerful. It impacts all of us.

Rather than striving to lessen its effects in clinical trials, a far better investment might be to develop strategies to amplify its impact. Why not utilize the natural power of our brain, our thoughts, our bodies for good?

There's also something much darker, called the nocebo effect.

The nocebo effect occurs when patients are given negative expectations about what might happen during the course of their treatment. And it is just as impactful.

It's what was happening to me each night as I awaited the medication. The very sight of the administering nurse made my brain start to anticipate what was about to happen. It began to prepare for nausea.

In those same medical trials, if people were warned that there might be side effects to the drug they were being prescribed, even the group of people who received the placebo experienced these side effects. Nausea, fatigue, trouble sleeping. All occurred without any scientific reason in the control group.

Our expectations aren't something to be taken lightly. They effectively shape the world in which we live and what happens in it.

Do you want to create healing and vitality and positivity? Or do you want to remain mired in negativity?

It's time to retrain our brains to utilize the power of expectations in the way that we desire.

To stop negative forecasting about what will happen, and instead relearn what it means to expect amazing.

If I Only Had a Brain

The brain hates uncertainty.

Uncertainty wastes energy and time as our brain sorts through all the possible outcomes of a situation. If our prehistoric ancestors had to constantly shift through all the possibilities as a potential threat approached, we wouldn't be here.

Instead, our brains are wired for efficiency, as we've discussed. Thus our brains draw from previous experiences and make educated guesses about what will happen. And while it saves our brains time and energy, it also traps us into telling ourselves stories that sometimes just are not true.

In his fascinating book called *How to Change Your Mind,* Michael Pollan explains this phenomenon: "We approach experience much as an artificial intelligence (AI) program does, with our brains continually translating the data of the present into the terms of the past, reaching back in time for the relevant experience, and then using that to make its best guess as to how to predict and navigate the future."[2]

In other words, our brains literally go back to what has happened in the past to *guess* what is going to happen in the future. So if something went poorly in the past, your brain wants to convince you that it will go poorly in the future to eliminate the uncertainty that it hates.

And while of course good things have also happened to us in the past, we often recall negative events more than positive ones, as a form of protection.

Yeah, your brain is working against you.

But what if we could reject our brain's mental shortcuts and start to reprogram our thoughts?

What if we could discard the negative expectations and adopt the lens of a young child who expects everything to be awesome?

What if you could harness that sense of expectancy and use it to your advantage?

With four kids and a demanding travel schedule, I wanted to pause to remember and celebrate the person who matters to me the most: my wife.

I think many of us wonder if we'll ever find someone to spend our lives with, someone who will come to know who we actually are, and somehow choose to love us anyway. I was certainly no different. I spent many years worried about whether or not I would find someone to love me. With scars ravaging my body, a noticeable limp when I walk, and no fingers, that was a very real fear when I was a little boy. It was a reality that I lived with for more than a decade after the fire.

I fell for Beth the very first time we met in college. She's stunningly beautiful and a blast to be with. After three years of friendship, a period of time during which I asked her out repeatedly and was rejected repeatedly, she finally realized we could be something more. In a twist of fate, one I remind her of frequently, it was Beth who eventually asked me out.

I was of course attracted to her beauty, but what I loved the most about Beth was her heart. She was unpretentious, nonjudgmental, humble, focused, and faithful. I remain amazed that she chose me, married me, and loves me.

But even a guy who understands how good he's got it can lose sight of that fact. Life can get in the way and cause us to forget to treasure the very things that we know in our hearts are priceless.

So on January 1, 2017, I bought a new journal, opened it to the first page, and wrote the words "Dear Beth."

What followed was a note from me, committing to her that each night for the next year, instead of missing out on how good our life was, or focusing on something that went wrong, I would record something *she* said, *she* did, *she* shared that was remarkable. I wanted to capture, in the midst of the busyness of our lives, not only how fortunate we were but how remarkable she was, every single day. I no longer wanted to take her for granted.

So, without her knowledge, each evening I wrote down something beautiful that she said, she did, or that we experienced together. I wrote about enjoying coffee on our screened-in-porch, our walks around the neighborhood together with our dog, the way she glowed as she descended the steps in an evening dress before we headed out for a special event.

I recorded the little things she did to get the kids to practices or prepared for tests, the baskets of dirty laundry that magically appeared cleaned, folded, and placed in drawers each night.

Some of the entries were deeply private, moments shared between a husband and wife. Others were hilarious moments experienced with family or friends. But each night I recorded something wonderful about her, lest it become forgotten or overlooked.

The longer I did this practice, the more of her kind acts I noticed. The cataracts of daily living and missing what matters most were removed; my eyes were opened to the marvelous ways my wife improved the lives of all of us around her.

A gift intended for her became one for me.

On December 25, 360 days after the journal journey began, I handed her the poorly wrapped gift as our kids played excitedly with their new toys.

She unwrapped the package to discover a well-traveled, scuffed, coffee-stained leather journal. She opened it and saw my handwriting as well as movie-ticket stubs, receipts from restaurants, plane tickets from a special trip we had taken together, and a simple love note she had written to me and hidden in my bag before a trip for work. As she turned the pages she saw several hundred entries tracking our year together.

As the kids played on obliviously, with Christmas music whispering in the background, tears filled her eyes and a smile graced her lips.

"John, this is . . . amazing. But, why? Why did you do this?"

I took her hands in mine and sat down next to her on the couch.

"Beth," I said, my voice cracking with emotion, "I began to realize how much I took you for granted. I didn't want it all to pass by unacknowledged and uncelebrated. I see what you do every day to make my life better and our kids' lives possible. I love you and wanted you to know it."

She gave me a huge hug.

First-time love.

First-time living.

And it was alive and well in our living room on that Christmas morning.

Listen, relationships are hard. Try adding four kids to the mix, and our busy lives are even harder. Visit our home some night around dinner and you'll get a sense of how taxing daily life can be. There are bills to pay, dishes to wash, laundry to put away, homework to do, practices to schedule . . .

It is not always perfect, is often chaotic, and can start to feel a lot like work.

And the very person that you chose as your partner in the journey of life can start to seem like a mere support player, if not an obstacle who isn't carrying their weight or doing something the way *you* would.

The very life that you dreamed, hoped, prayed, and worked for can start to feel more like drudgery.

When I started that journal, in preparation for each day's entry, I was actively looking for Beth's kindness, her support, her empathy, her patience, her beauty. I was seeking it out, expecting it. And that sense of expectancy opened my eyes to everything that was already there in the first place.

Sure, sometimes your partner won't pull their weight or will do something that upsets you. And if you look for that, you'll find it. Many of us become experts at this.

Or you can look for the many ways they are doing the best they can, going above and beyond whatever you could have imagined.

Same day. Same experiences. Same chores and responsibilities and chaos. But one perspective drains the love and joy out of a relationship and the other magnifies it.

Look for good and find good.

Look for bad and it will show up.

The concept is transformative in a romantic relationship, although the excercises of seeking the good in others, tracking their actions, expecting the best, and recording the journey apply in every facet of life.

What could this kind of positive expectancy do for your job? For your interaction with your kids? For your drive to work today? For the corporate meeting later this morning?

Listen, it requires great effort to take hold of the powerful sense of expectancy to stop assuming the worst, and to instead expect to see the best.

But in looking for it, tuning into it, tracking it, recording it, and sharing it, we are radically changed by it.

You see, our expectations shape our world.

My advice?

Expect amazing. Expect beauty. Expect awesome. Expect joy.

It will dramatically influence what you see. And what happens next.

12

The Joyful Awaiting

OH, MARILLA, LOOKING FORWARD TO THINGS IS HALF THE
PLEASURE OF THEM. . . . YOU MAYN'T GET THE THINGS
THEMSELVES; BUT NOTHING CAN PREVENT YOU FROM HAVING
THE FUN OF LOOKING FORWARD TO THEM. . . . I THINK IT
WOULD BE WORSE TO EXPECT NOTHING THAN TO BE
DISAPPOINTED.

L. M. Montgomery, *Anne of Green Gables*

Getting kids to bed can be an exhausting, time-consuming venture.

In our house, the journey begins with getting them into—and then out of—a bathtub. From there, the assembly line includes drying them off and getting them to pull on their pajamas, brush their teeth, and comb their hair. There's a quick straightening of their room, laying out their clothes for the morning, and picking a book to read.

Once in bed, we read a book, or sometimes I tell them a funny story, and then we pray together.

While I was tucking Henry into bed recently he attempted to stall the inevitable.

After having already read "just one more story" several times, I leaned over, kissed his forehead, stood up, turned off the light, and made my way out of the room.

Just a few steps down the hallway, I heard his voice call out, "Dad?"

I ignored it, hoping he would fall asleep. Don't judge. I had three more kids to get to bed and a desire to spend some uninterrupted time with my wife!

"Dad?" he called again, even more emphatically.

A mix of guilt and an excuse to spend another moment with my little guy sent me back.

"What is it, buddy?"

He looked up at me. "Dad, how many days until my birthday?"

His birthday is December 7. This conversation was taking place a couple of weeks after Christmas.

I wanted to respond, *Henry, way too freaking many days to count! Now go to sleep.*

But instead I moved further into his room, sat on his bed again, brushed back his hair, and responded, "Great question." I assumed he'd be pretty disappointed when I added, "Your birthday is about 340 days away."

He looked away for a moment. I could see his little mind doing the math, working it out, thinking it through.

He then looked back at me and said, "Awesome. Tomorrow can we make a countdown calendar to get ready for it?"

His birthday is more than eleven months away, and this kid wants to get ready for it?

My friend, *this* is the power of joyful awaiting.

Kids can't wait for the next big thing. They are always looking forward to the next holiday, the next weekend, the next vacation, the next sleepover. And it's not just the big stuff they enthusiastically await.

It is why they can sit cross-legged watching through the glass on the oven door as the chocolate chip cookie dough transforms into cookies. It's why they wear their swimming trunks to bed when they know they are headed to the pool with a friend in the morning. It's why, when learning their birthday is 340 days away, they respond with fervor and joy, preparing for the countdown.

Children intrinsically know how sweet it is to thoroughly anticipate something. But you don't need to be a kid to experience it.

Have you ever watched the face of a groom as his bride walks down the aisle? Or witnessed someone hold their grandchild for the first time? Have you seen the smile of an Olympian perched on top of a platform preparing to receive her gold medal? Have you ever been present the moment a unit of soldiers is released from their ranks to finally rejoin their families after a fifteen-month deployment?

The delight that emanates from joyful awaiting is a beautiful part of life.

In fact, research shows we get more enjoyment out of something after we've had time to anticipate it. One such example was noted by George Loewenstein, a professor in economics and psychology at Carnegie Mellon University and director of the Center for Behavioral and Decision Research. He performed a study asking respondents: If they could receive a kiss from anyone they wanted, would they rather have the kiss today or three days from now?

Which would you choose? Well, the vast majority of respondents chose three days from now.[1] They wanted something to be excited about. They understood the promise of joyful awaiting.

Anticipation, it turns out, is one of the things that make life so rewarding.

As I walked out of Henry's room that night, I remembered my own countdown, thirty years earlier.

Joyful awaiting helped me survive five months in the hospital.

Each day, Mom would arrive in the midafternoon, Dad around dinner. We'd talk or watch television or just sit together as a family. But between strictly enforced visiting hours and their need to navigate the responsibilities of parenting five other kids, each evening would end in heartache.

The clock would slowly tick toward 8:00 P.M. A nurse would enter my room, reminding them that visiting hours were almost over.

I'd beg them not to leave, plead with them to please come back, and eventually cry myself to sleep. Only nine years old, I was tied down to a bed, in indescribable physical pain, struggling emotionally, in a dreary hospital room, by myself, and it felt as if my parents were abandoning me for the night.

One evening as visiting hours came to an end, Mom reminded me that we were climbing a mountain. That a time would come when we wouldn't have to say goodbye, when we'd leave this room together, for good.

When? How many more days?

My parents' eyes met. After more than a month learning all about burn care and the challenges that remained in front of me, my parents knew another dozen skin-grafting surgeries had to be scheduled. Each one required a week of healing before the next. My dad walked over to the calendar that hung on the wall. After a little math, he flipped to May 26, took out a pen, put a large X on the page, and wrote below it in large letters: HOME. Then he counted how many days remained until that fateful date.

From that night forward, every evening before they left, I asked, "How many more goodbyes until I get to go home with you?"

The countdown started with 114 days. Then 113. Each night we'd see that number ticking down and the dream of home moving closer.

This nightly countdown did little to reduce my anxiety of being left alone, or the physical pain that I experienced. But it made a massive impact on my outlook. It set before me a goal, a dream, an expectation: Of getting better. Leaving here. Going home. Being with my family.

Of returning to normalcy.

On a Saturday morning in late May, my dad walked into my hospital room for the final time. He was pushing a wheelbarrow full of LifeSavers candy and bottles of champagne as a token of appreciation for the efforts of the staff. It was a celebration. There were tears, hugs, toasts, and lots of smiles.

But as we left that room that final time, we weren't surprised.

We'd been expecting it.

Joyful awaiting doesn't ensure what we are going through will be easy. It just provides the conviction that the reward and the wait will be worth the struggle.

Don't leave your expectancy dormant.

Wake it up and see the adventure unfold.

Sense #2: Expectancy

It's all downhill from here.

Or

A great adventure awaits.

My friend, before you lie two paths.

On one, you see the downward slope.

You don't know exactly what's coming,
but you expect recessions,
layoffs,
health setbacks,
and disappointments.

You know your best days are behind you.

You wish you could just turn around and go back.

On the other, a magnificent mountain appears in the distance.

You can anticipate the epic view from the top.

You see there will be challenging terrain to get through,
but also believe you've got the strength to get through it.

Fueled by the immense power of hope,
you know that the destination will be worth it.

You get to choose
which path you traverse from here.

Adventure awaits for those who seek it.

Stop acting ordinary, pack your glove, and unleash
the power of your expectations.

Immersion

Cultivating Your Attention to Be Fully Engaged in Every Moment

IT IS QUITE POSSIBLE THAT AN ANIMAL HAS SPOKEN CIVILLY TO ME AND THAT I DIDN'T CATCH THE REMARK BECAUSE I WASN'T PAYING ATTENTION. CHILDREN PAY BETTER ATTENTION THAN GROWNUPS. IF FERN SAYS THAT THE ANIMALS IN ZUCKERMAN'S BARN TALK, I'M QUITE READY TO BELIEVE HER. PERHAPS IF PEOPLE TALKED LESS, ANIMALS WOULD TALK MORE. PEOPLE ARE INCESSANT TALKERS—I CAN GIVE YOU MY WORD ON THAT.

E. B. White, *Charlotte's Web*

immersion:

(N) THE STATE OF BEING FULLY ENGAGED, ABSORBED, AND PRESENT IN THE WORLD SO THAT YOU CAN SAVOR THE GIFTS ALL AROUND

13

Missing What Matters

IT IS ONLY WITH THE HEART THAT ONE CAN SEE RIGHTLY;
WHAT IS ESSENTIAL IS INVISIBLE TO THE EYE.

Antoine de Saint-Exupéry, *The Little Prince*

"You missed it, Daddy."

It was early on a Saturday morning when my five-year-old son, Jack, whispered those sad words into my ear.

I'd returned late the night before from a weeklong whirlwind speaking tour and was still exhausted from the travel. Over the previous seven days I'd been in eight states and delivered more than a dozen presentations. This morning I was jet-lagged, wiped out, and in desperate need of more sleep.

Next to me, my wife was beginning to stir as Jack's whisper grew in volume. "Daddy, wake up! You missed it!"

I had no idea what he was talking about. Was it a baseball game? Had I inadvertently missed his birthday?

Nope. It was something much simpler but no less important.

Over sixteen years of marriage, Beth and I have moved three times. With each home, we've been blessed to have a grand magnolia tree tower over our front yard.

As a guy who travels a lot, I've been to Washington, DC, when the cherry blossoms are in full bloom. I've stared straight up in awe at the redwoods north of San Francisco. I've hiked through the Costa

Rican rainforest, basked under Hawaiian palm trees, and heard the whispering magic of aspens in the mountains of Colorado. Yet my favorite tree remains the magnolia. And my favorite experience is playing with my family below one as it blossoms.

The official harbinger, in our household, that spring is arriving is when the glorious white, pink, and purple blooms unspool overhead, the magnolia aroma rains down, and the great tree comes to life.

The morning Jack woke me I was in my bed, lying next to my wife for the first time in a week. The kids were a bit bigger. Beth was a little more tired.

And the magnolia tree in our front yard, which had been dormant all winter, had awakened, sprung to life, fully blossomed, and dropped its petals.

It's an event I get my kids fired up about every spring. It's a display that symbolizes perfectly the promise of new life. It's an awesome spectacle.

And I missed the entire show.

My work requires a good bit of travel. There will occasionally be things that I miss. Many of you can probably relate.

But sometimes do you feel like you're missing it and you haven't even gone anywhere? Times when you are physically present, but emotionally absent? That life is happening all around, but you aren't really present? For any of it?

Take an everyday scene at the park. Kids are thrilled to be there. They are making new friends, playing in the sand, sailing high on the swings, or lost in a game of make-believe. They may be a bit too loud and get a little dirty. But they are laughing, running, engaging with friends. Savoring the moment.

Now, pivot your attention from the kids and the playground to the benches surrounding it. What do you see?

On the sidelines of the park, sit the adults. Their heads are bent. Their thumbs are swiping, scrolling, tapping. Every now and then, someone glances up at the sun in frustration. They tilt their phones, trying to see their screens.

Their focus is on something else, somewhere else, far away.

And it isn't just when we're at parks. From family dinners to corner diners, from airport terminals to team meetings, you'll see proof: There exists a vast chasm between our physical presence somewhere and wholehearted engagement once there. Since becoming obsessed with social media, email, texts, headlines, and Angry Birds, with every beep, we excitedly grab our phones, check the screens, thumb our replies, and swipe right. And all the while, we miss out on whatever we are doing, and the people we are actually with.

We were not made to be in a thousand places at once.

We were made to be here, in this moment, right now.

No one exemplifies this the way children do. When we are young, we don't understand the concept of time. There is only the now. As a result, children are completely absorbed in what they are doing. The rest of the world falls away as they become engrossed in activities they love: building with their Legos, looking at a book, coloring a picture, digging in the mud.

This is the gift of childhood. Total immersion in what the world has to offer.

And then there's us, the adults. We are halfway present for every meeting, barely aware of what we're eating, hardly watching the television show. We are on our devices, or worrying about tomorrow, or stewing about yesterday. We are constantly in rewind or fast-forward, rather than play.

Far from being absorbed by what's in front of us, we're barely even here.

To live In Awe, we must wake up: Each moment we experience—from the sunshine in the park to the brainstorming meeting in the conference room to the commute at the end of the day—can become significant only when we give it our full attention.

Only then can we stop missing the marrow of life.

Wake-Up Call

In my late twenties, I spent several years working part-time as a hospital chaplain. One visit remains seared in my memory.

The patient was an elderly gentleman suffering congestive heart failure. As I sat at his bedside, we chatted about baseball, his failing health, and how he felt looking back over his life.

Seeing the youth fresh in my face, he thought perhaps he could impart some advice.

"John, talk to me a few years ago, and I'd tell you about all I accomplished in life. I'd tell you about the business I'd built, the successes I celebrated, the effort required and the payoff received."

He paused and coughed. His breathing was labored, and the simple act of speaking required a Herculean effort.

"But along the way, I also sacrificed some things in the pursuit of that success," he said. "I put in so many hours that I barely saw my family. I claimed to be doing it all for them, but in the attempt to build a better life, I lost my way. I turned my back on what's truly important. Eventually my wife left me. My kids barely know me."

I felt his loneliness fill the room. I didn't know what to say.

He took a deep breath and sighed. "John, I spent a lifetime sprinting up the ladder"—he paused and looked out the window—"only to discover after making it to the very top, I had the damn thing leaned against the wrong wall."

I'll never forget that last sentence or the dispirited tone with which he delivered it.

Now, let me be clear: I love climbing ladders. I partner with organizations to increase revenue and profitability. I speak with audiences to wake them up from accidental living, to encourage them to pursue big goals, and ultimately lead lives of impact. Climbing the ladder isn't the problem.

The problem is when the effort to ascend higher keeps us from noticing where we are and why we're climbing in the first place. The issue is when we are so focused on the next rung, the next step, the next goal, that we become blind to the blessings of today.

I'm not suggesting we put the ladder away. But it's time to pay attention to how we spend our days and where exactly we are climbing. To examine what success truly looks like and how to most effectively engage in this moment.

That's all we really have.

Our greatest fear should not be whether we will climb high enough or fail at what we're doing or fall from the top. No, our greatest fear should be succeeding at the stuff that just doesn't matter.

It's time to reawaken our sense of immersion so we can stop missing what matters. It's time to relearn how to be fully present and connect with those we love, the work we do, and the life we lead.

Time is finite. And how we choose to spend it matters profoundly.

Because nothing is more painful than gaining the world at the expense of losing the very things that matter most.

14

Future Focus

YOU PILE UP ENOUGH TOMORROWS, AND YOU'LL FIND YOU
ARE LEFT WITH NOTHING BUT A LOT OF EMPTY YESTERDAYS.
I DON'T KNOW ABOUT YOU, BUT I'D LIKE TO MAKE TODAY
WORTH REMEMBERING.

Meredith Willson, *The Music Man*

I'd just finished speaking to a group of young entrepreneurs.
Chatting with enthusiastic attendees as they filtered out of the
room, I saw a young woman approach. She introduced herself as
Stephanie and shared a challenge that she was facing.

"I'm stressed out all the time. I'm not sure what the trigger is, but
all day, and every day, I feel the entire weight of the world resting on
my shoulders." She looked away with a pained expression before adding: "I think it's beginning to suffocate me."

I asked Stephanie to tell me a bit more. She began to describe her
life, how her day starts early, with meetings at 7:15 A.M. She nor-
mally packs a lunch because there's rarely more than twenty minutes
to eat. With additional meetings that fill her afternoon schedule, on
good days she gets home around 6:00 P.M., but several days a week the
meetings occupy her until eight. After getting home, she has a quick
dinner by herself (because her family already ate), tackles a couple
more hours of work, and makes a list of things she needs to get done
the next day. After a quick check of social media, she falls into bed
around midnight.

I got exhausted just hearing her describe it all! No wonder she was feeling stressed and suffocated.

Yet there is a detail I left out.

The meetings Stephanie had in the afternoons and evenings weren't budget meetings or sales calls, but extracurricular activities and practices.

The work she did after dinner wasn't data analysis for an IT firm, but homework for her classes.

This woman wasn't an executive climbing a corporate ladder, but a fifteen-year-old sophomore in high school with her eyes focused on the very first rung.

As we chatted more about why she was so busy, Stephanie told me that she participated in eight different clubs in addition to playing two sports.

I asked her if she liked the activities she participated in.

"No, not really."

"So why are you doing all of this?" I asked.

"Because I want to get into a good college. With any luck, something Ivy League."

"Why?" I asked.

She looked at me, confused. Why would I ask something with such an obvious answer?

"Well, the college I attend will impact my career opportunities."

"So then what?" I asked.

She stared at me again, as if the answer was obvious.

I mean, isn't life all about securing a highly paid job from a prestigious company, and fighting for promotions and raises and accolades until you've reached the top? Isn't life about leaning in and crushing it at every turn, and winning the race?

Maybe.

But for many of us that marathon climb leads to burnout, disappointment, disillusionment, and exhaustion. Not to mention our lives can end like that gentleman I mentioned earlier, looking back on it despondently, wondering what it was all for.

Now, I'm not insinuating it isn't valuable to be hired by a world-class organization and be paid well for work done. I get that grades matter, that extracurricular activities are beneficial, that higher education is important. Top-tier universities may very well provide greater access to exciting research and a remarkable network of peers.

It is worth noting, though, that many of the finest executives I meet credit their success to humble beginnings. Do you know how many CEOs from today's Fortune 100 companies attended an Ivy League college?[1] Just fourteen.

Stephanie, not yet old enough to drive, three years away from being able to vote, embodies a phenomenon that is spreading like wildfire through our culture today: We exchange the magnificent gift of youth for the misguided notion that it should be utilized to set us on the right academic and career path.

Hoping that the right college will lead to the perfect job.

And that the perfect job will lead to a perfect career.

And that the perfect career will lead to a perfect life.

But what if in exchanging what we actually love today for some vague notion of a perfect tomorrow, we forfeit the joy of living immersed in this moment and the chance to live In Awe each day?

Yes, we all need money to live, food to eat, shelter over our heads. We desire fulfilling, purposeful work where our talents and the world's needs collide.

But if we are too future-focused, we forget how to live In Awe today.

And the trouble doesn't start in high school.

Let's examine what has happened to youth sports in the past couple of decades.

Youth sports have become a multibillion-dollar industry that is larger than the entirety of the National Football League.

What started as play in the backyard with neighborhood kids has been transformed into an industry that pushes four-year-olds into soccer clinics, seven-year-olds into traveling sports teams, and ten-year-olds into Tommy John surgery to repair ligament damage due to overuse.

Seated on foldout chairs on the sidelines, parents complain about the intense investment of their time and money. They grumble about the loss of lazy weekends and the sacrifice of family schedules.

But who signed their child up? Who wrote the checks for the $10,000 that many families pour into these sports annually?

We invest ridiculous amounts of time and resources in the hopes that our child won't miss out on anything, and may even be one of the few who receive a scholarship for their hard-won skills.

Yet only 2 percent of high school athletes actually receive those coveted awards.

So we fill their schedules and free time with activities that wear them out and teach them that it's all about where they are going. Today's happiness is something we sacrifice for the future. But what will their future truly look like?

Though I didn't meet Stephanie's parents, I can imagine what their lives might entail.

Managing kids and two careers, they are in constant motion from sunup to sundown. It starts first thing in the morning when they get out of bed and check their phones for urgent messages before heading down to get lunches packed, breakfast fixed, and kids out the door.

At work, they shift continually from meetings to email to conference calls, barely having time to do the actual "work" that drove them to their industry of choice.

They pick up dinner while wrapping up one more conference call, get home and summon the kids who are home to the table, eat quickly, then send their kids off to homework and bed. They half-watch a show while still checking work email and social media, before falling exhausted into bed.

Now, that may be a bit of an exaggeration. But just a bit.

We have lost our ability to focus on the moment in front of us, giving it our all and getting the most out of it.

A few years ago, I took a vacation with my family. For ten days I stepped away from work completely, untethered myself from technology, and instead played on the beach with my children. One evening after dinner, I was playing a fierce card game of War with my oldest, Jack. He looked up at me, and said, "I sure like having you around."

I stared at him in surprise. While yes, I travel a lot, and my days are spent at the office when I'm not traveling, what I think he actually

meant is that for those ten days, I was giving him my undivided attention. I wasn't looking at my laptop or cellphone. I wasn't torn between all the other demands on my life. I was just there with him.

It jarred me awake.

What if success was not about getting someplace, but about experiencing each of the moments leading us there?

So. Let me ask you a different question.

Have you had enough?

Turning the Tide

Father Tom Hoar asked me that question when he joined me on my
Live Inspired Podcast. He has committed his life to helping people recover from alcohol addiction. He believes their answer to this question is the key to determining whether they are truly ready to move
in a new, life-giving direction.

Have you had enough?

If the answer is no, then Tom lovingly encourages them to come
back at a later time. For those who answer yes, Tom begins walking
with them down the path of recovery.

Because Father Tom only works with those who answer a re-
sounding yes to his question, an astonishing 70 percent of his clients
stay sober after they leave.

Their answer to that question is the key.

Tom knows the struggles of addiction intimately. Despite his calling, to cover up feelings of inadequacy, he found himself drawn to
alcohol in moments when he was alone. One night, despite the fact
that he was the on-call chaplain for the fire department, he began
drinking yet again. And then the phone rang. He was needed down at
the station to counsel a family. He responded to the call—and fielded
questions about the smell of alcohol on his breath.

He went home that night, and stared at himself in the mirror.

He saw large bags under his eyes and disheveled hair. He felt his
heart still racing and realized what he most desired would never be
discovered at the bottom of an empty bottle.

He looked deeply into his own eyes and asked, "What the f*%# are you doing?"

And that was his last drink. He'd finally had enough.

Change happens when we've had enough of the life we're living and long for something better.

When we realize the addiction we're chained to isn't satisfying the need.

There is a mighty addiction we universally wrestle with today.

We are addicted to the unimportant.

We are missing the miraculous to stay tethered to work, the media, social media, on devices that steal our attention away from the moment in front of us.

So have you had enough?

Of responding at all hours to requests that could most definitely be handled tomorrow?

Of giving your attention to the nitpicky tasks that can hijack our lives?

Of counting down to that vacation, when you'll finally be able to relax and enjoy your family, only to find the demands of work have followed you there, too?

Of working so hard toward some future that you've forgotten how good you have it today?

If the answer is yes, then it's time to get off the treadmill of the tyranny of the urgent. To learn what it means to take things one at a time.

15

Work. Play. Rest. Repeat.

"WHAT I LIKE DOING BEST IS NOTHING."

"HOW DO YOU DO NOTHING?" ASKED POOH, AFTER HE HAD WONDERED A LONG TIME.

"WELL, IT'S WHEN PEOPLE CALL OUT AT YOU JUST AS YOU'RE GOING OFF TO DO IT, *WHAT ARE YOU GOING TO DO, CHRISTOPHER ROBIN*, AND YOU SAY, OH, NOTHING, AND THEN YOU GO AND DO IT."

"OH, I SEE," SAID POOH. . . .

"IT MEANS JUST GOING ALONG, LISTENING TO ALL THE THINGS YOU CAN'T HEAR, AND NOT BOTHERING."

A. A. Milne, *The House at Pooh Corner*

There are many days my wife and I feel like grossly underpaid Uber drivers.

With the activities, practices, playdates, and school functions of four children, we often find ourselves driving them all across St. Louis.

My favorite time is the morning commute to school. All four, fastened into their seats, radio off, sun rising. A little focused time to ask them questions about their days, plans, friends, lives.

Some days it's like four songbirds singing behind me, sharing and laughing and engaging. Other times I have to repeatedly turn around to make sure they're still there because it's so silent.

No matter the level of interaction I receive, something peculiar happens when we arrive at school.

After the car comes to a stop, the doors open, the kids pop out, the doors shut. They put on their backpacks, turn away from the car, and run.

They run.

No, not away from school! These kids sprint *toward* their school, that massive brick structure packed with teachers, pop quizzes, and spelling tests.

What in the heck are they running toward? What happens in school that is so awesome, so amazing, so engaging that they feel the need to sprint to get inside?

Can you imagine that same type of enthusiasm in your life?

When was the last time you ran not because you were late or might miss your flight, but out of anticipation?

Yeah, me too. It's been a while.

But there is something inherent in the structure of the school day that draws children to enter that building with enthusiasm. Once attendance is taken and quizzes handed out and a lesson delivered, the bell rings.

And that bell is important.

It signifies that homeroom is over and it's time to move on, to science, or English, or social studies. When the bell rings again, it's time to move to another classroom and another period. Later the bell rings for recess. Then for math or gym. Then it's lunchtime and recess again! Time to enjoy a little break.

Each day is organized into short bursts of focus and activity.

Teachers recognize that kids can't and shouldn't sit at a desk all day long, for hours at a time. Instead, there is a beautiful cadence to the day, that allows for periods of intense work, and then a break, followed by a period of regenerative rest and joyful playtime.

Work, play, rest, repeat.

Children don't work while resting. They don't try to eat while playing. They do each thing, fully immersed in it, and then move on to the next.

It's not rocket science. But it's far from our reality as adults.

If you're like me, you probably ate your lunch while catching up on email. Hopped on a conference call while you drove to work. Caught up on reading that report during your kid's baseball practice. And can't even remember the last time you took time to actually rest.

But I want to suggest something. What if all the stress that we feel as adults comes not from all that we have on our plate, but from trying to get it done at all hours of the day?

If we go back to how we acted as children, doing one thing at a time, and then moving on to the next task, the next stage, the next moment, we would rediscover our sense of immersion: your ability to be so fully present and tuned in to a task that everything else falls away.

One of the great thieves of joy is simply not being present to the task at hand.

My friend, I want you to try pausing here.

Read the sentence above again. Let it wash over you. Absorb you.

One of the great thieves of joy is simply not being present to the task at hand.

Now, I understand *why* we multitask. Most of us feel as if we are forced to do more and more at work, at home, and in life. But we still have the same twenty-four hours a day. If we have more responsibilities but the same amount of time in which to do them, we had better try to do more than one thing at a time, or we'll never get it all done, right?

But multitasking is not what our brains were made for.

And it has dire consequences.

Brain Break

One of the reasons we, like Stephanie, feel stressed and suffocated is because our brains are begging for a break.

Stanford neuroscientist Daniel Levitin studies what happens to our brains during the kind of task switching that is now a normal part of our daily lives. And what he discovered is that when the brain is forced to switch back and forth between different tasks, it uses its energy (oxygenated glucose) much more quickly, leaving the brain literally starved.[1]

When you feel spent, depleted, and burnt out, there is a physiological reason for that. Your brain needs a break.

A study at the University of London found that subjects who multitasked while performing cognitive tasks experienced a severe drop in IQ. The decrease was essentially on par with what you'd experience after smoking marijuana or missing a night of sleep.[2]

Ouch.

And yet we seem to think that multitasking is what the best of us do. Who has time to do one thing at a time anymore?

But the constant filtering of information leaves our brains downright depleted.

We can't even relax without multitasking. A whopping 88 percent of us use a second screen while watching television.[3] I know I'm guilty of this! On an average weeknight, you'll find me answering a few work emails with the television on in the background. But to our brains, this isn't relaxing. As our brain shifts between demands, trying to figure out where to focus its attention, we are exhausting it even further. Rather than zoning out and giving our brains a rest, we are adding additional stress on an already fried system.

It's time to stop the madness.

Wouldn't you like to stop striving and climbing and responding, and actually remember what it feels like to enjoy life?

Wouldn't it be awesome to once again be so completely absorbed in each moment that our days are no longer a long slog to get through, but a series of moments to savor?

Here is the new formula taken straight from our children:

When we work, we work.
When we play, we play.
When we rest, we kick off our shoes, put up our feet, and actually give our brains a break!

Remember the kids running in to school? We too can start each day with excitement and exuberance. We've just got to relearn an old dance.

Stop doing all things at once.
Allow yourself to go deep.
Do one thing at a time.

16

Hang It on the Fridge

IN EVERY JOB THAT MUST BE DONE,
THERE IS AN ELEMENT OF FUN.
YOU FIND THE FUN AND SNAP!
THE JOB'S A GAME.

**Robert B. Sherman and Richard M. Sherman,
"A Spoonful of Sugar"**

Every day I spent in the hospital was sectioned off into little pockets of torture.

There were the brutal ninety-minute bandage changes.

Thirty-minute sessions of speech therapy.

Sixty minutes of occupational therapy.

And then the most painful part of the process, an hour of physical therapy.

For those of you who have had to recover from a painful injury, you know just how excruciating physical therapy can be. In my case, the extent of my injuries demanded the rehabilitation of every joint in my body. It was a critically important component of my healing, and led me to be able to return to life fully. Enduring it, however, was agony.

I began the sessions in my wheelchair, then moved to yellow therapy mats on the floor, and concluded each session in a broom closet far away from other patients. The therapists took me there so that no one could hear my screams.

The sessions continued for more than a year after I was released from the hospital. My parents or a family friend would drive me to the hospital, drop me off at the physical therapy wing, and pick me up an hour later.

Besides knowing that my torturers would eventually tire and move on to the next victim (I mean, patient!), there was something else I looked forward to that got me through those difficult sessions: seeing my friend Scott.

Scott worked at the valet stand.

When he saw this nine-year-old kid wrapped with bandages, eyes reddened from the physical therapy session he'd just endured, Velcro-strapped into a wheelchair, waiting for a ride home, he must have recognized that this kid needed some extra attention.

Although Scott was incredibly old (a nineteen-year-old is ancient in the eyes of a nine-year-old), he would take time away from his job to keep me company. He would pull a chair alongside my wheelchair, look out at the driveway filled with emergency vehicles and we'd pretend all those ambulances were part of our army and that we were planning an ambush. Scott was my sergeant, and I was his lieutenant. He took orders from me.

For a little boy who had a team of doctors, nurses, and therapists always telling him what to do, it was a welcome reversal.

When my ride finally arrived, Scott would do one more thing that always made my day: He'd let me talk on his walkie-talkie.

He'd hold it in front of me, push the talk button, and say, "Okay, we're live. Go for it!"

With great enthusiasm I'd say, "Johnny to base. Johnny to base. Send reinforcements. Enemy approaching. Over and out."

We'd laugh uncontrollably as some angry security officer would hop on and yell: "Kid, get off the radio!"

With tears no longer in my eyes and a big, beaming smile on my face, I would be wheeled by Scott toward my parents' car and he would help me in and tell me he looked forward to seeing me the next day.

It doesn't seem like that big of a deal when I look back on it. They were, after all, just small moments of kindness. Yet to a struggling child, they made a huge difference.

Scott was a college student, trying to earn some spending money for the weekends. But even at that age, he knew that work wasn't just about putting in the time and picking up a paycheck.

He knew that any job, when performed with excellence, could become something greater. He knew there were no insignificant people, that small acts mattered and little things made a big difference.

I believe every job we do matters, and all work is sacred. But too often, we can get caught up in busywork and neglect the essential life-giving work begging to be attended to. Sometimes we must turn away from the demands and instead focus on what truly makes a difference.

The kind of work that makes us immensely proud.

Remember when you were little and were excited about something you created? What words would you say as you took it from your backpack and handed it to your parent?

Look what I made!

I still hear those words from my children every time they create art, whether at school or our kitchen table. They smile broadly, hand their picture to me, describe the scene they created, and light up as I compliment it. Before walking over to the fridge to hang it up proudly, they do one more thing every artist does after completing a masterpiece.

They put their name on it, to claim it as theirs.

When was the last time you walked out of work feeling that kind of satisfaction?

When was the last time you finished a project, printed your name on the bottom of it, ran to your boss, assistant, or colleague, put it on their desk, and pumped your fist, proclaiming, "Boom! That's how you crush an Excel sheet, baby!" or "That's how you teach the Pythagorean theorem, my man!" or "That's how you do a patient hand-off to afternoon staff!"

Why not?

Why are these statements laughable instead of commonplace?

Rather than depicting a workforce pumped up about their work and enthusiastic about their progress, a 2017 Gallup poll reported that just 33 percent of employees felt engaged in their work.[1]

I may not be great at math, but I'm pretty sure that means most of us feel the opposite, despite the fact that we are putting in more and more hours at the job.

So we're working more, but getting less out of it.

That's not a recipe for living In Awe. It's a recipe for burnout.

Martin Luther King Jr. wrote extensively about the sacred value of work. He reminds us of the immense opportunity it holds for each of us:

> When you discover your life's work, set out to do it so well that the living, the dead or the unborn couldn't do it better. And no matter what it is, never consider it insignificant because if it is for the upbuilding of humanity, it has cosmic significance. And so if it falls your lot to be a street sweeper, sweep streets like Raphael painted pictures. Sweep streets like Michelangelo carved marble. Sweep streets like Beethoven composed music. Sweep streets like Shakespeare wrote poetry. Sweep streets so well that all the hosts of heaven and earth will have to pause and say, "Here lived a great street sweeper, who swept his job well."[2]

Any work we do, when we do it well, has cosmic significance.

I love that.

Do you feel this way about your work? Are you sweeping streets like Raphael painted in your sales job, in your role as a custodian, or at your position in middle management?

Why couldn't you? Some of us miss the possible joy and profound impact inherent in our current job because our thoughts are focused on another one. Far from being fully immersed in the calling of this job, we get fixated on another kind of job, maybe one with pedigrees and prestige, and it leads us to chase status instead of significance, like Stephanie did.

Yet research shows that one of the greatest indicators of job satisfaction is not the kind of job you have but instead, the conviction that your work matters.

A recent study from researchers at the University of Michigan revealed that hospital janitors who believed their job was a form of healing were much more enthusiastic about their work than those who thought they were simply there to clean. Because they believed their role was essential to the healing process, they walked into work each day understanding that their job had significance.[3]

The job remains the same no matter your perspective. Recognize its value and impact, and you'll be more satisfied. Stay focused on how it is just something to pay the bills, and you'll find it drudgery.

When I was in the hospital, from the janitor to the valet, the entire medical team knew, not only their task to complete, but their underlying mission. That their jobs mattered, and mattered profoundly.

And it saved my life.

Not just in healthcare, but in all industries, we must return to the heartbeat of our work.

The fact remains that what we do each day can truly change lives.

To get back in touch with work that feels significant, we have to stop focusing our efforts on "low-value garbage."

I got that phrase from my friend Juliet Funt. She is the founder of WhiteSpace at Work, a company that helps us recognize how we spend our time in the workplace, so that we can enjoy our work more and get more satisfaction from it.

White space is "a strategic pause taken between activities." White space rejects the notion that our days should be spent reacting: to the call to return, or the email to answer, or the meeting to attend. Juliet suggests that by taking a pause, we can choose to turn to the kind of work that makes a difference, that allows us to feel deep engagement, and that actually matters.

Since our last conversation, I've become a practitioner of living white space. Between tasks, I'll walk over to the French doors in my office that lead outside, open them, feel the breeze, hear the leaves rustling, and do something most of us at work seldom do: think.

I know. It's kind of weird. At first, I was really nervous. *Man, I hope no team member walks in and sees me here . . . wasting my time . . . thinking!*

But I've found great power in letting my mind drift. How can we create a better way to do things if we never pause to analyze what we're doing in the first place? I no longer feel a need to apologize for investing time imagining a better way to impact, thinking of a cool guest to interview on our podcast; ideating around better ways to lead, write, or dream.

Our goal professionally isn't to simply be busy and active, but effective and productive.

We might equate those goals, as if they are similar, maybe even the same.

But they are vastly different.

Activity is staying busy: crossing off items on your list of calls to return or meetings to schedule. Trying to respond immediately to each email that comes your way. Low-value garbage.

Productivity is actually moving the needle on things that matter.

Far too many of our days are consumed with the former.

Yet what truly drives great results and deep satisfaction with work is the latter.

Companies have been striving to help us get immersed in important work. In 2008, Intel instituted a Quiet Tuesdays pilot program when, for four hours every Tuesday morning, a certain group of employees closed email, sent calls straight to voicemail, and shut their doors. They were free to get absorbed in creative tasks that required more concentration. Even employees who didn't have a creative task to turn to found that space helpful as a way to get back in control of their work schedule, instead of constantly reacting. They extended it to their entire staff.[4]

Jason Fried, CEO of BaseCamp and author of *Rework,* endeavors to ensure that this kind of time is carved out for his employees. Without it, he believes, they will never have the chance to access what he calls "deep work." Jason describes this kind of mindset as similar to the REM cycle of sleep. "That's where the good stuff happens, but it takes you a while to get into that zone. You don't just jump right into it. It takes you a while to get there. And if you are constantly being interrupted, you have to start over again."[5]

The kind of work that makes you want to hang it up on the fridge stems from the kind of work where you are fully immersed in what you are doing. Creative work that engages your whole being and feels deeply meaningful. Our constant onslaught of activity distracts us and prevents us from getting into the zone where the important work is done.

We have to stop the cycle so we can get back to the kind of work that lights us up, gives us confidence that our work matters. The kind of work that is worthy to hang on the fridge.

Put Your Name on It

Let me tell you about a guy I love named Brian Buffini.

Brian's family owned a painting business. It had been in the family for five generations. Throughout high school, Brian worked for his grandfather. His grandfather was a firm taskmaster who knew the way he got more business was by doing the current job to the best of his ability. You had to finish each job right and give it your all before you moved on. That's how you earned the best reputation and loyal customers.

At the end of the day, when his employees would report that their work was finished, Brian's grandfather would walk in to survey the site. And he'd ask a simple yet extraordinarily powerful question: *Can you put your name on it?*

Had you swept the floor? Carefully removed every remnant of painter's tape? Taken out the trash? Done the job so well that it was worthy of putting the Buffini name on it? It wasn't just you, but the reputation of five generations of your family on the line!

If the job wasn't done well enough to put the Buffini name on it, the employees would have to keep working. Because the Buffini name would only go on work completed with the highest of standards.

Brian took that commitment to excellence with him when he immigrated to the United States at age nineteen with a hundred dollars in his pocket. And it served him well. Starting with no network or capital, he grew into one of our country's top real estate agents. So many agents asked Brian how he achieved success that he began coaching them on how they could reach new heights. His organization has now trained more than 3 million agents in his strategies for taking a business to the next level.

And it starts with a "put your name on it" attitude. In other words, stay focused on the quality of what you are producing for your clients. Pay attention to how you are helping them into the home that is perfect for the next stage of their life. Provide excellence in all you do and realize that no job is too small to give it your all.

This kind of commitment can truly change lives. It can sanctify your experience of work and create a ripple that lasts long after the workday ends.

I was reminded of just how long that ripple can extend while at dinner with Beth several years ago. We were at one of our favorite restaurants, and Beth recognized someone she used to work with. While the ladies chatted, I introduced myself to the husband, Scott, and shook his hand.

He gave me a funny look. And then he asked: "Have you ever been a patient at St. John's Hospital?"

I looked at him with surprise. "Yes, why?"

The older man smiled and told me a story. "Years ago," he began, "I used to work there as a valet." My stomach dropped, as I looked at him through new eyes. He continued, "Man, I must have helped thousands of people over the years, but there was this one kid who I've never forgotten in the three decades that followed. A little boy named Johnny."

He looked at me and asked, "By any chance, was that you?"

I nodded and said:

"Yes, sir, sergeant. Glad to see you're reporting for duty."

We laughed and embraced, amazed that the bond between us felt as fresh as it had thirty years earlier. I confided in him how much those walkie-talkie sessions had helped me get over the pain of the therapy and remember that I was still a kid. How they'd lifted me out of the gloom of my recovery, and distracted me from the pain, the hard work, and the fact that I would have to do it all over again the next day.

I'd never forgotten his name. Or his kindness.

As we parted that night, and I reshared with Beth the impact he'd had on my life, I realized that Scott was able to see my need and respond accordingly because he wasn't wrapped up in busywork, or a checklist, or being the most productive employee. He was willing to be fully present and see the sacred work begging to be attended to.

What kind of impact could you have if you used the time put aside for the unimportant and ignored the checklist, and instead got immersed in the moment to see what sacred act was waiting to unfold?

To see the little boy who needs a reminder that despite how dire things look, there remains reason to hope, to laugh, to walkie-talkie for reinforcements.

We must make room for the good stuff. Let go of some of the *busy*. Focus on *important*. Then give it your all, and get that magnet ready to hang it on the fridge.

Because guess what?

Work isn't everything.

There's more to be done, if you remember to listen for the ringing of the bell.

When you work, work. Be all in. Lead courageously. Climb purposefully. Influence profoundly. Succeed wildly.

But when the bell rings, when the working day is done, recognize that it is time to do something else. Shut down the computer, put away the phone, get up from the desk, and race to the exit.

It's time for recess.

17

Go Fly a Kite

IF MORE OF US VALUED FOOD AND CHEER AND SONG ABOVE
HOARDED GOLD, IT WOULD BE A MERRIER WORLD.

J. R. R. Tolkien, *The Hobbit*

It was dark when I arrived, so the next morning, I hopped out of bed and threw back the curtains of the hotel to see the beautiful ocean just outside my window. I was there only for a day, but man, we just don't have the beaches in Missouri that they do in Hawaii. I couldn't wait to stroll down the beach and dip my toes in the ocean.

During my breakfast meeting, I met with some of the conference organizers, who had arrived a few days earlier to get everything prepared. I bounded into the room and asked, "Hey! How's the water? Is the beach as nice as it looks?"

They stared at me in confusion. Though they were squarely in paradise, not one had removed their shoes, shucked their sports coat, and stepped into the sand. Racing to get ready, they'd been too busy. No one had even looked out the window to notice the Pacific, just within reach.

Conferences are often jam-packed. Schedules get tight. There's too much to fit into each day.

But do you know what part of the school day is most essential for kids? What pocket of time matters most?

Hint: It's not math or science. It isn't reading or writing.

It is recess.

Active playtime allows what happens in the classroom to be much more effective.

A school district in Texas learned this firsthand. Like many other schools across the country, they were struggling to manage students who were being diagnosed with ADHD at increasingly younger ages and had trouble focusing in school. They decided to join a pilot program to see if adding more recess to the school day would improve student outcomes.

Modeling their program after the Finnish school system, which allows elementary school students fifteen minutes of unstructured, outdoor playtime for every forty-five minutes of instruction, the school shifted from providing just twenty minutes of recess for the kindergarten and first-grade students to four fifteen-minute recesses plus a lunch break each school day.

The teachers were initially concerned about the loss of class time, and how they would be able to cover all the required material. But halfway through the pilot year, one first-grade teacher said they were already "way ahead of schedule."

How could that be? They had less class time, but they were keeping pace and in fact moving more quickly through the material?

Here's what was happening. The students were less distracted and more engaged. They were less fidgety and making more eye contact with their teachers.

The class time was therefore much more productive.

The designer of the pilot program outlined the many benefits of more frequent recess. They included increased attentional focus, improved academic performance, improved attendance, decreased behavioral diagnoses, and improved creativity and social skill development.[1]

Not bad for a little extra time on the monkey bars.

Ohio State University pediatrician Bob Murray, who helped write the American Academy of Pediatrics policy on recess, says: "If you want a child to be attentive and stay on task—if you want them to encode the information that you're giving them in their memory—you've got to give them regular breaks."[2]

Kids need play to be at their best.

And it is just as essential for adults.

Many of the dramatic leaps we've made professionally aren't the result of working harder, but of stepping away and taking time to play. It allows our brains to get into the kind of state necessary to figure out new approaches to the problems we confront. Let me give you some examples.

George de Mestral, an engineer, stepped away from his desk one day to take a hike in the woods with his beloved dog. Upon returning home, he found his pants and his dog's fur covered with small green burrs that were incredibly difficult to remove. It was like they were glued to the fabric.

Being someone who loved to discover how things worked, he extracted one of the burrs and examined it under the microscope. It was made up of minuscule little hooks that grabbed on to any creature that passed by, embedding themselves into fabric or fur.

What George de Mestral created from what he discovered that day while out for a hike is what is known today as Velcro.

Alexander Fleming, while researching staphylococcus, a bacterium at the root of many infections, took several weeks off from his work to go on vacation with his family. Upon returning to his laboratory, he noticed that some fungus had grown in his absence, and that it had destroyed a colony of staphylococci.

He later named the mold penicillin. This accidental discovery would go on to give birth to a new class of drugs known as antibiotics, save millions of lives, and ultimately earn Fleming the Nobel Prize.

Oliver Smithies, a Nobel laureate scientist, famously loved to play. "His breakthroughs always came during what he called 'Saturday morning experiments.' Nobody was around and he could just play. 'On Saturday,' he said, 'you don't have to be completely rational.'"[3]

Regardless of our profession or age, we need play. Play permits us to get immersed in an activity we love, and enter a state of creative flow where we stop judging ourselves and start enjoying ourselves.

That's when revolutionary discoveries are made.

Tinker Time

Hanging in my conference room is a magnificent work of art created by my friend Russell Irwin. The work is titled *Ablaze*.

I reached out to him several years ago, explaining that I wanted to commission a piece of art that would symbolize both my journey and the unlimited potential within each of us. I wanted the piece to reflect that no matter how bruised or battered we become along the way, present adversity would not be wasted and the best remained ahead.

Russell and I got together for several conversations about what the piece could look like. Several months later, when he delivered the finished piece, I sat back just staring at it.

I wasn't expecting something so grand.

At a quick glance from a distance, the image looks like an oil painting of the sun, radiating light. Although it's stunning, that first impression completely misses the story of complexity, beauty, pain, and redemption told within the work.

The image isn't made with oil paints, but with *thousands* of pieces of colored paper meticulously glued down, then covered with other pieces of paper and more glue.

After the glue dries, Russell puts on a mask, and grabs a belt sander, laboriously removing layer upon layer of paper. It's a messy, loud, tedious process. When done with expert care, it reveals something that no other art possibly could.

Staring at it up close, you see that it's all a bit chaotic, torn, ripped, broken. It doesn't seem like it all fits together.

When you step back, though, the beauty of the image shines through.

As I stood looking at this incredible work of art that now graced my office wall, I asked Russell how he came up with this utterly novel approach to creation.

He laughed and told me a story.

One day he'd left his studio feeling stagnant and uninspired. He walked into his house to find his twelve-year-old daughter, Ashley, at the kitchen table, ripping construction paper to the size she desired, plastering the pieces with glue, and adhering them to a large sheet of paper.

Russell stood back and watched as beautiful artwork came to life from the shredded, mangled, sticky paper.

"Where did you learn to do this?" he asked, marveling at this new technique.

Ashley looked up, surprised by the question. "What do you mean? I'm learning it now."

And with that, she went back to her creation, back to making something completely fresh, original, and new.

She wasn't trained in a classroom. She didn't learn it from a textbook. In the very act of experimental play, she was creating something entirely new. She was revealing to her dad a technique that would transform his entire business. And she was joyfully lost in the moment.

When you get absorbed in a task and forget all sense of time and purpose, you enter a state called flow. It can happen when you are practicing a musical instrument or playing a sport. It can occur when kids are completely wrapped up in an imaginary game of their own creation. Flow is defined by a laser-like focus on one thing, and it's accompanied by the temporary deactivation of the prefrontal cortex, the part of the brain responsible for self-monitoring and impulse control. What that means is that, in flow, we turn off the annoying part of our brain that is worrying about what others think. This allows us to be less critical of ourselves and more courageous in action.

Consequently, we are also more creative.[4]

Flow, however, requires total immersion. You cannot access a flow state when constantly interrupted by email and texts and calls. This is the "deep work" state that Jason Fried wanted his employees to be able to enter. Play and work actually aren't that different when work is something creative and consuming. A quote often attributed to famed psychologist Jean Piaget says: "Play is the answer to the question: How does anything new come about?"

To live a life In Awe, we've got to relearn what it means to play.

We've got to recognize the call to look out the window, see the ocean beckoning, and go put our feet in the sand.

Play is not just about going to the movies, playing a board game, or going to parties on the weekends. Play is an attitude, where the only goal is fun or exploration or release. And you get lost in it.

And it is one of the most important elements of leadership.

I'll let historian Doris Kearns Goodwin explain.

Goodwin is one of the most respected presidential biographers of our time. In her most recent book she wrote about the leadership styles of four different presidents. These four presidents had something in common besides their exemplary leadership.

They all recognized the importance of play.

One of those men was Abraham Lincoln. In her earlier biography of Lincoln, Goodwin had recorded his dedication to the theater: "In the most difficult moments of his presidency, nothing provided Lincoln greater respite and renewal than to immerse himself in a play." His assistant said of Lincoln, "The drama by drawing his mind into other channels of thought, afforded him the most entire relief."[5]

Respite and renewal and relief. Doesn't that sound appealing?

But you don't need to reserve a weekend at the spa to achieve this. It is available to every one of us when we take the time to play.

Teddy Roosevelt understood this, too. He famously went swimming every afternoon. His fifth cousin, Franklin Delano Roosevelt, another president, threw parties. These were the most important leaders in the country, shouldering more responsibility than you and I will ever know. And they made sure that they still had time for fun, even during the most difficult moments. *Especially* during the most difficult moments.

Goodwin stated: "If Lincoln during the Civil War can go to the theater a hundred times, and if FDR during World War II can have a cocktail hour every night where you can only talk about books you've read and gossip, and if Teddy Roosevelt can take two hours every afternoon to exercise," she says, none of us has an excuse to skip incorporating play into our lives. "We just keep thinking our time is more complicated. It is because we've made it so."[6]

So now it's time to make life a bit less complicated and a lot more fun. It's time to unapologetically step away from work and skip to recess. Our recess can mean reading a book, painting a picture, or attending a sporting event. It can include taking a hike, going for a run, or playing a game with your kids. Recess doesn't mean you don't work hard or take life seriously. Instead, it means you'll actually enjoy what you're building and be equipped to build it even better.

So get out to the blacktop, pick up your tennis racquet, go fly a kite, or jump some rope. Give your brain the break it deserves.

Play will unleash greater creativity, connectivity with others, and ability to leverage the power of flow.

And it will give you a chance to do something else incredibly important.

Nothing at all.

18

Look Up at the Clouds

"WELL, AN OLD STUMP IS GOOD FOR SITTING AND RESTING.
COME, BOY, SIT DOWN.
SIT DOWN AND REST."
AND THE BOY DID.
AND THE TREE WAS HAPPY.

Shel Silverstein, *The Giving Tree*

One evening we couldn't find Patrick.

It was approaching dinnertime and everyone else was in the kitchen, but he was nowhere to be found.

I called upstairs, "Patrick!" But there was no response.

When that didn't work, I did what any calm parent might do: I screamed louder. Then much louder.

Realizing that even my sternest voice wasn't working, I went upstairs to get him. But he wasn't there. After checking throughout the house, I went outside.

There, in the backyard, I saw him sitting in an Adirondack chair.

The trivial anger I'd felt during my search faded as I made my way over to him. I sat down next to him, put my arm around him, and asked, "What are you doing, Patrick?"

Without even looking over at me, he replied, "Nothing." With a contented smile on his lips.

He made me realize that sometimes I get so focused on getting things done, propelling the day forward, and checking all the boxes that I miss the gift of simply being in the moment.

But Patrick knew what he was doing. He'd spent the day at school, hard at work, and he was about to engage in more activities. So it was time for a rest.

When was the last time you sat in the middle of the day, without your phone, without an agenda, with nothing to do?

When was the last time you weren't worried about getting something accomplished, going through some checklist, or preparing for the next meeting?

The University of Michigan scientists who propose that we have mental fatigue due to our constant multitasking believe that what allows our brain to rest is something they call "soft fascination."[1] Soft fascination is the state your brain enters into when you watch a sunset or gaze out at the horizon, the kind of meditative trance that occurs when you are transfixed by a campfire or watching rainfall. Finding opportunities for soft fascination inside may be hard, but nature provides countless prospects.

You can gaze at the leaves blowing in the breeze.

Stare up at the clouds passing by.

Watch water tumble over rocks in the creek.

In fact, nature does much more than provide opportunites for your brain to rest. Doctors up to date on research on the curative effects of nature are beginning to prescribe it as a remedy for what ails us.

Neuroscientist Oliver Sacks said that gardens and music were two of the most important non-pharmacological therapies available. "I cannot say exactly how nature exerts its calming and organizing effects on our brains, but I have seen in my patients the restorative and healing powers of nature and gardens, even for those who are deeply disabled neurologically. In many cases, gardens and nature are more powerful than any medication."[2]

Fresh air, gentle breezes, and the sounds of birds can be life-giving for us.

Exposure to nature has been connected to improved mood in those struggling with depression. It reduces stress. Yoshifumi Miyazaki, a physical anthropologist and a proponent of *shinrin* therapy (the Japanese art of forest bathing), revealed that walking in a forest, as opposed to an urban environment, delivers:

- A 12 percent decrease in levels of cortisol (the hormone that causes us to feel stress)
- A 7 percent decrease in sympathetic nerve activity (which governs our fight-or-flight behavior)
- A 1.4 percent decrease in blood pressure
- A 6 percent decrease in heart rate

These life-giving and restorative benefits are discovered by simply going outside.[3]

"Forest bathing" does not mean just taking a walk. It means practicing the art of immersion, allowing all of your senses to notice what they are experiencing. You awaken your sense of smell and breathe in the aroma of pine needles. You listen to the whispering wind caressing leaves high above. You look at the deep green of the moss on the far side of the tree. You take off your shoes and feel the mud, cool on the soles of your feet.

You stop dipping your toes. You go in, deep.

While this practice is gaining widespread popularity throughout the world, even spending just twenty minutes in a park, whether you take a walk or simply sit on a bench, can make you feel better.[4]

When we bring rest back into the rotation, we are able to recharge our batteries so that we can more fully show up in our relationships, our work, and the world.

I'm sometimes traveling to three different cities in a week. Because of all the travel, and the fact that I try to get home in time for dinner to see my family as much as possible, I often take early morning flights so I can get there and back in the span of a few hours. That means getting up at 4:00 A.M. So sometimes I'm running on very little sleep, fueled by a little brown beverage served by a barista.

I'm not alone. Thirty-three percent of Americans are getting six hours of sleep or less per night. For some, how little they sleep becomes a badge of honor. Because of course, there is so much more important stuff to do, right? We're that important. Only those who don't have real responsibilties have time for sleep.

But the research would argue otherwise.

It doesn't take a rocket scientist to recognize that sleep and rest are restorative.

And guess what? If you are getting less than six hours of sleep per night, you are 30 percent less happy than your colleagues who went to bed on time!

If only we would listen to the admonition we yell at our kids: Get to bed!

Sleep also helps with engagement on the job. Getting less than six hours of sleep each night was one of the best predictors of burnout in the workplace.[5]

Commit to sleeping more than six hours tonight, and you'll find yourself 30 percent happier, and more satisfied with your work! It's a pretty good deal, isn't it?

We think our problems are so complicated—and sometimes they are. But just twenty minutes spent outside in the open air and a little more sleep can make a prodigious difference.

So rest improves your happiness, helps you perform better, and increases your engagement.

A sixty- to ninety-minute nap can improve memory test results as much as a full eight hours of sleep. Ernst and Young conducted a study in 2006 and discovered that for each additional ten hours of vacation their employees took, their year-end performance improved by 8 percent. Those who took vacation were also less likely to leave the firm.[6]

I probably don't have to tell you that in America, we aren't so great at taking vacations. Despite the fact that we get just ten vacation days on average, 55 percent of Americans don't even use all of them.

What happens on vacation? We rest. We play. We get outside. We explore new places, inviting the mindset of first-time living back into our daily experience.

And yet, too many of us leave that opportunity behind to stay productive and get more stuff done.

To get back to living In Awe, we must recognize the importance of rest. When we do, we'll be happier, less burnt out at work, and more available to others.

But that's not all! Rest also does something else even more valuable.

It reminds us of what's truly important.

Reset

It's time to bring back the Sabbath.

Now, I'm not suggesting that we need to follow a certain religion in order to learn to rest. But I do think that the practice of stopping that is woven into the fabric of many religions is something we desperately need in our secular lives.

With fewer Americans participating in regular religious services, combined with new technology that allows us to work 24/7, our culture no longer has anything to remind us to make time for weekly personal renewal.

More than a decade ago, I read an article by author Judith Shulevitz that moved me so deeply I cut it out of the paper. When I started the *Live Inspired Podcast,* I knew that I wanted her to be one of my guests, to impart some of her wisdom with our listeners. As we talked, she shared that being raised in a traditional Jewish home meant she had observed the Sabbath religiously as a child. The practice of stopping the traditional routine from sundown on Friday to sundown on Saturday made time for something important.

They paused work.

They came together as a family.

They united as a community.

The Sabbath was a time for adherents of the Jewish faith to follow the example set by God, who after six days of creation, rested on the seventh day. It was once such a widespread concept among Christians that there were laws requiring stores, banks, and museums to be shuttered on Sundays so that everyone could observe the holy day.

Today, most stores are open, and we get irked when one isn't.

We use the day to hammer out the slew of tasks that have been waiting for us all week long. Laundry. Grocery runs. Soccer games. Maybe a few hours spent getting ahead of the workweek to come.

Judith was once guilty of this, too. As she grew up, she moved away from not only her faith but also its traditions. She worked hard during the week and packed her weekends with activities. There was nothing left in her life to remind her to stop and relax, to enjoy a meal with friends, to sit down and read a book.

Judith ultimately found her way back to her faith and the Sabbath tradition. The pause that the Sabbath required was so incredibly restorative and life-giving to her that she became an evangelist for it. For Judith, the Sabbath has less to do with being religious but more to do with emphasizing the value of setting aside time to step away from action so we can remember why we work so hard.

"Why should God have considered it so important to stop?" she asks. "God stopped to show us that what we create becomes meaningful to us only once we stop creating it and start to think about why we did so. . . . We have to stop to remember."[7]

There is power in the pause.

When was the last time you stopped all the striving and organizing and productivity to ask: What am I doing all this for?

Our culture's attempt to right this wrong? Offer one more task as a solution, of course! Today you'll find apps that remind you to meditate and offer courses on mindfulness. But unfortunately, these solutions frequently become just more of the problem: They get added to our to-do list, one more task to accomplish.

Instead, I believe we need to appreciate what it means to truly stop. Sit. Stare up at the clouds. And do nothing. Absolutely nothing!

Take a nap, or get lost in our thoughts. Become skilled in what Patricia Hampl, author of *The Art of the Wasted Day,* described as "the lost music of wondering, the sheer value of looking out the window, letting the world float along. It's nothing, really, this wasted time, which is how it becomes, paradoxically, charged with 'everything,' liberated into the blessed loss of ambition."[8]

The blessed loss of ambition: This is what rest can be. We sacrifice the constant striving and we allow ourselves to relax into the space of nothingness.

No agenda.

No problem-solving.

No productivity.

In doing so, I promise you'll be reminded of what life is truly about.

Put that on your to-do list.

Then sit back and give yourself permission to do exactly that: nothing.

19

It's Your Job

YOU KNOW THAT PLACE BETWEEN SLEEP AND AWAKE, THAT
PLACE WHERE YOU STILL REMEMBER DREAMING? THAT'S
WHERE I'LL ALWAYS LOVE YOU. . . . THAT'S WHERE I'LL BE
WAITING.

Hook, directed by Steven Spielberg

"Do you go by Mitch or Mitchell?"

"My friends call me Mitch."

"Then I'll call you Mitch. Because I hope by the end of this semester that you will consider me your friend."

As a freshman at Brandeis University, Mitch Albom was so inspired by Professor Morrie Schwartz that he registered for a class with him every semester. The professor even asked that Mitch call him "Coach."

Upon graduating, the student gave his professor a leather briefcase as a token of his appreciation. Schwartz gave Mitch a hug, and then a final assignment: "Promise me you'll stay in touch."

Mitch made the promise. And then broke it every day for almost two decades.

After graduation Mitch Albom became an award-winning journalist, an ESPN broadcaster, a daily radio show host, and a prolific writer. One Friday night, Mitch sat on his couch, flipped on the television, and stumbled upon an episode of *Nightline*. Ted Koppel was sharing the story of how a seemingly ordinary professor with the terrible diagnosis of amyotrophic lateral sclerosis could remain so positive, so generous, so alive.

Mitch was overcome with emotion when Koppel shared the name of the professor: Morrie Schwartz.

The following morning he tracked down his old friend's phone number and called. When Morrie answered, Mitch awkwardly said, "I don't know if you'll remember me. My name is Mitch Albom."

Dying with ALS, but still exuding life, Morrie responded lovingly, "Why didn't you call me Coach?"

The following Tuesday Mitch flew from where he lived in Michigan to visit with his favorite teacher at his home in Newton, Massachusetts. After a long visit recounting the lives both had led in the eighteen years since their last visit, Mitch asked if he could come back and visit Morrie next week.

He kept the promise this time.

Mitch continued his visits every Tuesday for the next several weeks. His beloved professor was just as inspiring, if not more so, as he lived the final days of his life. Realizing that his expenses were mounting, and that the lessons he was receiving during each visit from his dying friend might teach others how to live more fully, Mitch asked if he could write a book about their conversations.

Morrie couldn't imagine people being interested in his life and death, but agreed to it.

Even with Mitch Albom's media connections and significant platform, every publisher turned down the seemingly dark, tragic story of an old teacher dying of ALS. Finally a single publisher, Doubleday, agreed to make the gamble, printing twenty thousand copies.

During my visit with Mitch, I was shocked to learn how difficult it was for him to get published. Because, in the twenty years since its publication, *Tuesdays with Morrie* has been translated into forty-five languages and has sold more than 14 million copies.

In one of their final visits, Mitch, observing how generous his teacher was with everyone who came into his room, struggled to understand how he could be so giving.

"Coach, why are you so kind, so patient, so present with everyone? How do you keep giving to all of us, even though you are the one dying?"

Morrie looked over to him and responded, "Taking makes me feel like I am dying." There was a long pause. The simple act of breathing now required significant effort on Morrie's part. He then added, "But giving . . . giving makes me feel like I am living."

It was one of the final lessons from his coach, and it dramatically altered the arc of Mitch Albom's life.

After the immense, surprise success of *Tuesdays with Morrie,* and remembering Morrie's advice that "living was giving," Mitch Albom today actively supports more than a dozen charities and runs an orphanage in Haiti.

Although Mitch and his wife, Janine, never had children of their own, they came to view the almost four dozen orphans at Have Faith Haiti Orphanage as a blessed opportunity to expand their family—and to shower the kids there with love and affection.

But they never expected that one of those children would profoundly change their lives.

That child was Chika.

She was born three days before the 7.0-magnitude earthquake that devastated her country, killing 300,000 people and leaving 1.5 million people without shelter. She and her mother found themselves homeless. A year later, her mother died in childbirth and Chika went to live with an aunt. At age three she was brought to the orphanage and into Mitch and Janine's care.

Chika had bright, vibrant eyes, a permanent smile, and an easy laugh. Her joy for life was infectious. When Chika turned five, however, she began to exhibit troubling symptoms, and she was taken to the hospital in Haiti for an MRI. Whatever illness she had was beyond the scope of what they could diagnose and treat, and the doctors asked if there was any way she could be treated in the United States.

Mitch and his wife arranged for Chika to come to Michigan, and soon learned her diagnosis: an inoperable, irreversible brain tumor called diffuse intrinsic pontine glioma (DIPG). DIPG is a cancer of the brain stem that is aggressive and debilitating. It affects just a few hundred kids each year. There is no curative treatment.

The Alboms didn't want to send Chika back to Haiti to die. So they decided to try to give her a chance at life. They brought her home to live with them while she underwent six weeks of radiation.

They had no idea that their lives would be forever altered by the presence and love of this little girl.[1]

Real Work

Having spent her entire life in Haiti, Chika considered everyday things here as absolutely miraculous. Hot water coming out of a faucet. An elevator ride. Even in the midst of her hospital treatments, Chika found moments of pure joy.

As time went on, the little girl who danced through life lost her ability to walk. Mitch began to carry her.

When Mitch developed a hernia, his doctor asked him, "Are you doing a lot of lifting?"

Mitch laughed. "Yes." He was instructed to stop, but he refused. There was nothing as rewarding in his life as being able to carry this little girl.

One day he and Chika were coloring. He looked at his watch and realized he was running late for work. Mitch hurriedly stood, raced to grab his items for work, and bent to give Chika a kiss goodbye. The little girl looked up, surprised.

"Where are you going?" the now seven-year-old demanded.

"I have to work."

"I don't want you to go."

"Well, it's my job."

"No, it isn't. Your job is carrying me."

Mitch stared down at Chika, who had brought so much into his life. He thought about what she'd said, and what was truly important. He put down his briefcase, sat next to her, and began to color.

Mitch describes himself as having been a bit unbalanced before he reconnected with Morrie. He was goal-oriented and ambitious. "Time was a commodity to be given away in exchange for advancement."[2]

But Morrie awoke in him the real point of living. And now Chika gave him another crash course in what was truly important.

Mitch and Janine immersed themselves in their real job for the final weeks of Chika's life, tenderly cuddling her, rocking her, feeding her, and loving her. When she could no longer speak, they would lie next to her and tell her stories or play dolls with her.

Eventually the brave little girl took her last breath this side of eternity.

And at her side were Mitch and Janine, weeping, brokenhearted.

But not angry.

"How can we be angry?" Mitch told me. "We did not lose a child. We were given one."

Chika lived well beyond the twelve months she was expected to. For twenty-three months, she transformed the Alboms' lives. She gave them a purpose, a sense of joy, and the opportunity to love someone in a way that they'd never experienced before.

Throughout those twenty-three months, they knew what their job was: to love that little girl and give her a shot at life.

It was a job that they embraced with open arms. A job they were immersed in for those months she graced them with her presence. A job that changed their lives forever.

Mitch acknowledges the deadlines he missed, the opportunities he lost, and the money he did not make during those many months. But he wouldn't change a thing about how he spent that time with Chika.

He was living out Morrie Schwartz's edict. For that period of time, he devoted his life to that little girl, and he had never felt more alive.

Sometimes we get confused about what our job truly is.

Is our primary job at the workplace we clock in to every morning? Is our most important duty to make money, balance spreadsheets, and hit sales targets?

Or is our job to love our family and friends? To give to our communities? To fully show up, totally engage, and spread joy and love in each portion of our days, whether we are working, playing, resting, or just being?

What is your job in life? Are you giving it the care and attention it deserves?

I hope that you never have to face the dire diagnosis of a loved one in order to realize how much you are missing, and recognize that it is time to wake up to the phenomenal gift of immersing yourself totally in every moment, in every interaction, every day.

To live, in other words, like Chika.

20

What Time Is It?

IT'S ALWAYS TEA-TIME.

Lewis Carroll, *Alice's Adventures in Wonderland*

There are times in life when work does take over.

For an accountant it may be during tax season. For farmers it may be the planting and harvest seasons. For a pediatrician it may be flu season, when her waiting room is bursting with sick kids. For an author, it is most certainly the few weeks before and after a book is published.

The book tour celebrating the release of *On Fire* led to dozens of interviews on radio, television, and podcasts and a speaking schedule that included a different city every day for fifteen consecutive days.

Knowing this would be a busy season, Beth and I agreed to say yes to it.

Yes to the travel, the time away, the distraction from being fully engaged at home.

And yes to the resulting stress on both of us.

In the midst of the two-week book tour, I returned home for eighteen hours before a flight back out of town. We went to church as a family; I made breakfast for the kids and enjoyed a little sacred time together. After chatting on the screened porch with Beth and shooting baskets with my boys, I went into the house to shower and prepare for the week ahead.

While packing some shirts in my suitcase, I heard the pitter-patter of footsteps. I turned around, and a few feet away stood my four-year-old, Grace, her blond hair pulled back, a large pink bow atop her head, her blue eyes twinkling. She greeted me with a bubbly, beautiful smile and a simple question: "Daddy, will you have a tea party with me?"

My flight was in less than ninety minutes.

I wasn't packed.

I needed to change.

There were files to grab and things to do.

It just really wasn't the right time.

So what did I do? I bent down, looked her in the eyes, smiled, and said, "Sorry, Grace, I don't have time. Next time, when I'm back."

Are you kidding me?

I looked into those beautiful, soulful blue eyes, grabbed that little hand, and practically shouted back, "Yes!"

Instead of packing a bag, I ate crackers and poured imaginary tea.

Instead of writing about leadership, we talked about princesses.

And instead of missing it because I was getting ready for my week, we enjoyed the gift of an ordinary, special moment.

I believe one of the secrets to real success, sustained happiness, and genuine inner peace is recognizing what time it is.

The famed philosopher William James, who lived at the end of the nineteenth century, when there weren't today's gadgets to demand one's attention, wrote: "My experience is what I agree to attend to . . . without selective interest, experience is an utter chaos."[1]

My experience is what I agree to attend to.

What a wise, thoughtful way to put it.

Yes, we can attend to the emails accumulating. We can attend to the news on TV. We can attend to the to-do list, the laundry, or our chores.

Or.

We can attend to the important.

We can savor the moment. Our children playing. The sun peeking over the horizon. Sipping a mug of coffee while sitting on the porch on a summer morning. A lazy visit with an old friend, talking about anything and nothing.

To live In Awe, we've got to remember to focus. Unless we consciously choose where we place our attention, our experience will disintegrate into utter chaos.

Work.

Play.

Rest.

Repeat.

See what that new cadence can do to your life.

Sense #3: Immersion

Is it time to attend to the unimportant?

Or

Is it time for tea and the things that are essential?

My friend, stop zombie-walking through life,
tethered to tiny gadgets, staring down at what doesn't matter.

Put them down.

Then open wide your eyes and your heart.

Go outside.

Take a breath.

And ask yourself: What time is it?

Is it time to work? Play? Or rest?

Then go and immerse yourself fully in whatever ensures
that your ladder is leaning against the right wall.

Climb high, go deep, be engaged.

In relationships. At work. In play. And during rest.

There is so much life to be savored,
if you just give it your attention.

Your experience is what you agree to attend to.

You get to choose.

When you choose wisely, you'll rediscover the joy
that has been waiting for you all along.

Living fully immersed is, after all, your job.

It's time you act like it.

Belonging

Opening the Gift of Truly Letting People In

GENERALLY, BY THE TIME YOU ARE REAL,
MOST OF YOUR HAIR HAS BEEN LOVED OFF,
AND YOUR EYES DROP OUT AND YOU GET LOOSE
IN THE JOINTS AND VERY SHABBY.
BUT THESE THINGS DON'T MATTER AT ALL.

Margery Williams, *The Velveteen Rabbit*

belonging:

(N) THE SENSE OF COMFORT, PEACE, AND JOY THAT COMES FROM THE KNOWLEDGE THAT YOU ARE WORTHY, YOU BELONG, AND YOU ARE AN ESSENTIAL PIECE OF THE PUZZLE

21

All Better

WHEN GIVEN THE CHOICE BETWEEN BEING RIGHT OR BEING KIND, CHOOSE KIND.

R. J. Palacio, *Wonder*

"What's wrong with your dad?"

When I heard those words, my heart sank.

I was picking up the kids from their first day of school, surrounded by dozens of other parents waiting for their kids to emerge from the building.

My boys were veterans on campus, children finishing their first days of fifth, third, and first grades, respectively. They knew the teachers, understood the flow, already had their friends. They had this thing covered.

Grace, our youngest, had just started kindergarten.

Our baby was leaving the safety and carefree days of early childhood for the rigor of full-day school. Not only would her days expand, her network of friends was certain to expand, too.

Apparently I was more emotional than Grace, because she'd already made a new friend. I watched as they came hurtling out of the school, arms locked, skipping.

I waved to get her attention; Grace waved back and guided her new friend over to me. With a massive smile on her face, Grace hugged me and handed me her backpack. She talked with the speed of an auctioneer, reporting the details of her first day, a radical departure from what I experienced with her brothers, who never shared more than a grunted "fine" or "good" before they headed off to play.

Grace's friend stood back at a safe distance, having never met me before.

As Grace continued chatting, I could see in her friend's face raw curiosity as she stared at me. Her eyes darted from hand to hand, her forehead furrowed, as a look of pained confusion settled on her face.

Then, with the sweet directness of a child, she pointed at me and asked Grace in a loud voice: "What's wrong with your dad?"

I knew immediately what the little girl was asking.

But Grace didn't understand.

She was so used to the shading on my face, and the unnatural curve of my hands, that she'd never even considered that something might be wrong with me.

I'm just her dad. I've always been this way.

Confused, she looked back at her friend and said, "What do you mean?"

The little girl responded, "His hands look like puppy dog paws."

After hearing her friend's question that day on the playground, five-year-old Grace looked up at me. Her big white bow held back her blond hair; her pink-rimmed glasses framed her sparkling blue eyes.

She then turned back to her new friend and, without any semblance of embarrassment, shame, or anger, responded: "Nothing's wrong with my dad. He just got burned when he was a little boy. But he's fine now. He's all better."

Her friend looked down at my hands, then up at my face.

Her suspicion faded.

Her face softened.

Acceptance settled in.

She smiled sweetly and said, "I'm glad you're all better."

Then she handed me her backpack and the two ran off to play.

Kids. They don't know not to point, stare, and gawk.

But they are honest. Unashamedly, brutally, and, this is the important part, beautifully honest. From *What's wrong with your dad?* to *Why is her skin that color?* to *Mommy, your stomach is like a soft, squishy pillow!* they say what is on their minds.

Yes, sometimes this leads to awkward encounters.

But their honesty also liberates them to enter into conversations that matter. What might first come across as judgment leads to understanding. They call out what makes us different, ask who we are, and wonder where we come from. Once their questions are answered, the confusion cleared up, the seemingly out-of-place explained, it's no longer an issue. They move on and get back to the important stuff.

Connecting.

Playing.

Living.

Loving.

In no other area can we learn more from our children than through their acceptance of others, and most important, of themselves. This doesn't mean they don't see differences. They do. But they don't ignore them. They don't shy away.

They engage.

They inquire.

They ask. They seek to understand.

Instead of being closed off and shut down, they have their arms open wide, and they meet the world with a transcendent willingness to see what it has to offer. They make friends, invite and spread love, and feel like the world is a big, beautiful playground filled with potential playmates.

They are still in touch with their sense of belonging.

As someone who is familiar with being different, I never mind when people ask me what happened to me. I mind much more when they do not.

In the hopes of being polite or not offending, adults tend to look away or ignore what makes us different. But what does that do? It builds a wall.

My friend, each time we look away, ignore, or assume, we add another brick onto a barrier that was never intended to be there.

It's time to return to the state where we knew deep down how connected we all are.

Pull Up a Chair

While speaking at the University of Southern California, I had the opportunity to meet a man named Augie.

Augie Nieto has lived with the brutal realities of amyotrophic lateral sclerosis for over ten years. Knowing the trajectory of the disease and the certainty of losing everything, Augie tried to take his own life shortly after receiving the diagnosis at age forty-seven.

He survived the attempt. And the experience ignited within him a deep desire to not only refuse to surrender to the disease, but to become a masterful example of abundant life in spite of it. He had the same spirit that coursed through Morrie Schwartz, who endured the same disease, and the same desire to still contribute, like Tempt.

We connected after my talk and spoke for almost an hour. I asked what the most difficult aspect of this brutal disease was.

He responded, "I . . ."

Augie sat motionless in a motorized wheelchair. Today he is unable to move any muscle other than the big toe on his right foot. Using technology he helped design, he's able to use his toe to type letters and communicate with friends.

"Don't . . ."

Augie was a pioneer and leader in the fitness industry before his ALS diagnosis. He founded, grew, and eventually sold the hugely successful brand Life Fitness. For Augie, fitness wasn't just work, it was life. He epitomized health and was a world-class athlete.

"Want . . ."

This one sentence had already taken him more than a minute to type. It was laborious, requiring all his mental effort and physical strength.

"To . . ."

He occasionally glanced over to make sure I was paying attention—and to let me know he was enjoying being heard.

"Be . . ."

At this moment someone approached thanking me for speaking. I asked him if he'd ever met Augie. He hadn't. The gentleman then stuck out his hand to shake Augie's. Augie stared back. After an awkward silence, the gentleman pointed at Augie, told him he looked great, turned, and walked away. As I watched the man exit the room, Augie finished his sentence.

"Ignored."

While he cannot undo his diagnosis and can't change his reality, he does wish one thing from those around him: "I don't want to be ignored."

What terrifies Augie is not the painful progression of ALS, or even the inevitable loss of life. It's that in almost every room he's in, people look past him, ignore him, or feel sorry for him.

We long to be seen.

We are a social species. We descend from tribes. We are wired for connection. We are created to go through life together.

So why aren't we willing to ask questions? To reach out a hand, open our hearts, and truly connect? About the good, the bad, and the beautiful parts of life?

It's because we don't want to expose ourselves.

In order to connect with others, we've got to let people in, instead of keeping them out. We've got to lower our guard and realize that, no matter what we're hiding, we still belong.

So instead of walking away, what if we pulled up a chair? Instead of shutting our hearts, what if we opened them wide?

It's time to tear down the walls that we have erected.

It's time to stop hiding who we are.

It's time to get back to seeing one another fully and celebrating who we are, so we can journey through life together.

22

The Contagion of Joy

I WISHED I COULD SPEND THE REST OF MY LIFE AS A CHILD,
BEING SLIGHTLY CRUSHED BY SOMEONE WHO LOVED ME.

Gail Carson Levine, *Ella Enchanted*

During the first week of February 2018, I flew from St. Louis to Miami, then out to San Diego, before heading back east with a late night arrival into Jackson, Mississippi.

As I prepared to board the plane for the final leg of the journey, I received a text from Tim, a dear friend back home. One of the financial advisors on his national sales team had shared some heartbreaking news in a weekly check-in: His neighbor's young son had been involved in a terrible car accident a few weeks earlier. The boy, just eight years old, had suffered a massive head injury, and was not expected to survive.

Shortly after the accident, the boy's parents were given a copy of *On Fire*. They were inspired by my story, and by the reality that miracles still happen despite dire statistics. *Could I reach out to his parents to offer support?* Tim asked.

I texted Tim back and asked him to track down their mailing address, so I could send a note and a care package.

After landing four hours later, I turned my phone back on. There was a detailed message from Tim providing the parents' names and phone numbers, and the mailing address of the hospital where their son, Curtis, was being treated.

I stared at my phone in shock.

That hospital was Memorial Hospital, in Jackson, Mississippi.

A chill went down my spine.

I had just landed in Jackson, a city that I'd never even been to before. I knew at that moment that this trip was about much more than a speaking event. That I needed to see this family in person.

Even though it was late, I reached out to the boy's parents, and scheduled a visit at the hospital the following morning.

After arriving, I made my way to the elevator and exited on the floor where Curtis was being treated and practically walked into his parents, Adrienne and Brad. They were anxiously awaiting Curtis's return from another early-morning surgery.

We sat down and began to chat. I learned that Curtis had been spending the weekend with his grandfather when they were involved in a serious single-car accident. The car was so demolished that when the first responders arrived on the scene, they rescued the grandfather and assumed their work was done. It was only after his grandfather asked how his grandson was doing that the EMTs realized there was a second person in the car.

They cut Curtis out of the car and airlifted him to Jackson.

He wasn't expected to survive the night.

When his parents arrived early the next morning, they rejoiced that he was still alive. And prayed that he could keep beating the odds.

Curtis had been fighting for his life for the last three weeks. He was still in critical condition, with extensive swelling of the brain. He still hadn't shown any real signs of life or purposeful movement.

I asked about his prognosis.

Brad took a deep breath. The doctors were amazed Curtis had made it this far. But they weren't promising anything. If he did pull through, there were likely to be lasting effects from his brain injury. They expected severe cognitive delays and thought it unlikely Curtis would speak again. He might never regain his sight.

I saw what the weight of this news was doing to his parents. But then Adrienne told me, "They can say what they want. I just want my son back. Regardless of his condition or how different he might be, I want the chance to keep loving my boy."

My eyes welled with tears. I couldn't imagine what they were going through.

With that, the doors to the elevator opened, and several nurses, doctors, and transporters emerged, pushing a hospital gurney.

Curtis was out of surgery.

The entourage stopped briefly to let Brad and Adrienne see their son.

The large gurney practically swallowed the boy. His light-colored hair poked out from a blue helmet that protected his skull against any further damage. Tubes tethered him to the machines that trailed behind him giving him a chance at life.

After a brief moment with their son, Brad and Adrienne let the medical team continue their journey down the hall. Curtis was pushed into the ICU, and the double doors shut behind them.

We stared despondently at those doors for a bit. It's wildly disheartening when your child is rolled away, out of sight, a picture of how completely out of control you feel.

I turned back to Adrienne and Brad, "He's a beautiful boy. I understand why you want him home. I bet his siblings are eager to see him, too."

Brad and Adrienne exchanged a look.

"They haven't visited yet," Brad said. "We don't know how they'll react when they see how much Curtis has changed. We don't want to scare them. And we're not sure Curtis would want them to see him like this."

I nodded. I understood their concerns. But also knew how lifesaving it could be to have your siblings by your side.

When I was stuck in a hospital bed for five months as a nine-year-old, no matter how severe my physical pain, how deep my sorrow, or how intense my fear, I knew that once a week, on Sundays, my entire family would come visit. I looked forward to it all week.

In the early stages of my recovery, when my eyes were still swollen shut due to all the fluids they'd pumped into me to cool my body temperature, my ears were anxiously listening for the sounds of their voices echoing down the halls. I have five siblings. Before the accident, all I'd wanted was my own room, my own space, and a little peace and quiet. Afterward all I wanted was my old life back. I longed for the noise, the raucous sounds of my family, and our messy, beautiful life.

Once the swelling subsided and I could open my eyes, their smiling faces reminded me how much I was loved. And after months of Sundays in my hospital room, when the staff finally allowed us to eat Sunday brunch together as a family in the cafeteria, it was as if new life was being breathed into me, sitting around the table with my family again. That dose of normalcy was vital. It reminded me who I was and all I was fighting for.

While everyone else was afraid to touch me, my older brother, Jim, would hug me every time he entered my room. My sisters Cadey, Amy, and Susan took turns gently rubbing my back to alleviate my pain. I remember being in my wheelchair, unable to move, when my two-year-old sister, Laura, came running down the ICU hallway (ignoring the admonishing nurses), climbed up onto my lap, and snuggled against me.

Now, don't get me wrong: Before I was burned, my siblings and I fought all the time. We wrestled, yelled, pouted, taunted, and tattled. And we returned to that same sense of normal the day I came home from the hospital! But during the months of recovery after I was burned, we set aside sibling rivalry and bickering to come together. The pats and back rubs and hugs and smiles didn't take away my pain, but they served as an awesome weekly reminder that we were going to get through this—together.

They gave me a palpable sense of belonging.

And that sense, sparked by their visits, just might have saved my life.

The Cuddle Cure

Why were the visits from my siblings so life-giving? Why did they inspire me to push through the week ahead? What is it about our connection with others that can fill our lives with purpose, joy, and meaning, and give us the will to continue on?

We are a social species, and our brains are wired for it. When you watch someone pick up a glass of water to drink, you can begin to feel thirsty yourself, thanks to mirror neurons. "We are hardwired to perceive the mind of another being," says Dr. Daniel Siegel, clinical professor of psychiatry at UCLA School of Medicine and author of *Mindsight*.[1] In other words, these neurons help us empathize with others in real time.

Neuroscientists believe mirror neurons helped our ancestors to survive. We needed a tribe to help protect us, find food, and provide shelter. Because we needed this interdependence to simply survive, we developed mirror neurons so that if one of the tribe members saw a threat to the tribe's well-being, the other members of the tribe would pick up on the fear and escape to safety, even if they couldn't see the threat themselves.

Think about that. Mirror neurons make our emotions contagious. It means that your mood can affect everyone else in the room.

I can be angry walking into my house, and without my saying a word, my kids are going to pick up on it. Or I can walk off a plane exhausted and full of anxiety and stress, and my colleagues are going to feel it, too.

Or I can walk into an auditorium and be fired up about life, and the audience can feel my excitement without me even saying a word.

In fact, Nicholas A. Christakis, a social scientist from Harvard, and James H. Fowler, a political scientist at the University of California, San Diego, found that you are 15 percent more likely to be happy if one of your friends is happy.[2]

It makes you wonder about the company you keep, right?

Our connections with others matter, and matter greatly.

When my siblings walked into my hospital room, they dispelled the worry and negativity and fear surrounding me, and instead brought joy. I'm sure my parents didn't enjoy managing five children of various ages in a hospital room with their son hooked up to tubes and machines and buttons that they shouldn't touch. But I'm so grateful they did.

They lifted my spirits. Gave me a sense of belonging, to dispel all the loneliness I felt in that hospital room.

And gave me something else that was just as life-giving.

While most people approached cautiously wearing hospital gowns and gloves, afraid to touch me lest they cause me pain or trigger an infection that could be deadly, my siblings raced to hug me. And in doing so, they helped me to heal.

Loving, physical touch does more than just feel good; it can possess healing properties. It has been proven to activate the immune system, lower levels of the stress hormone cortisol, and increase levels of the bonding hormone oxytocin.

We didn't always know this. We used to keep premature babies exclusively in their incubators in the NICU. But a study conducted in 1988 discovered that infants who were massaged for just fifteen minutes a day gained weight 47 percent faster than those who remained alone in their incubators, even though they were given the same amount of nutrients. The babies who were touched were also discharged from the hospital six days earlier than those who were not touched.[3]

Why? It goes back again to our early roots. When we are deprived of parental touch as children, our bodies think that we are on our own. Our metabolism then slows down to protect us because being alone means we don't know where our next meal will come from. And a slower metabolism stunts our growth in the long term.

Babies who are not held fail to thrive. While seeking to discover why orphanages were reporting infant mortality rates of 30 to 40 percent, researchers determined that a certain level of touch is required in order to turn on production of our growth hormones.

Today, we strive to place children under the age of five in foster homes, instead of bureaucratic institutions, because we have learned how important consistent, loving touch is to children. Institutions just don't have enough staff to keep up with human infants' need to be cuddled, snuggled, and rocked. Today, hospitals seek "cuddle volunteers" to visit the NICU so that babies can be held even when their exhausted parents need to catch up on rest.

And touch remains a powerful force for good long after our toddler days. A supportive touch from a teacher can double the likelihood of a student volunteering in class. A gentle massage from a loved one can decrease depression. Even a high five from a teammate can increase your connection to the rest of the team and improve chances of winning. Research shows that the most successful professional sports teams are those that touch the most throughout the game.[4]

Why?

Because touch helps us feel like we *belong*.

After listening to Brad and Adrienne's concerns about having their other children visit, I shared how the hugs and cuddles and handholding and love from my siblings might have saved my life. And encouraged them to bring Curtis's siblings to visit.

They thanked me for my advice. We exchanged phone numbers, hugged goodbye, and promised to stay in touch.

The following weekend I got a text from Brad. "Hate to bother you on a weekend. I wanted to share this video."

I eagerly clicked Play, and my screen began to show Curtis in an oversized hospital bed, blue helmet on, acting a bit agitated as he is being encouraged to sit up. The effects of his brain injury are evident. He still can't speak, or see. He doesn't smile. But it is clear he can hear the instructions of his parents. He is moving on his own.

From behind the camera, I hear Brad saying, "Curtis, your little brother and sister are here to see you."

Curtis's brother, age four, and sister, six years old, have been placed right next to him on the bed.

Curtis blindly reaches out with his right hand to find his siblings. He feels the body of his brother, and then reaches up to touch his face. As his hand feels the bangs of his brother, then his nose, a small smile of recognition appears on his face.

Curtis then rubs his four-year-old brother's face up and down, up and down, up and down, smiling all the while. And the entire time there is a look of peace, comfort, and connection on Curtis's face.

Overcome with emotion, Curtis stops patting his brother's face and uses his hand to begin wiping tears from his eyes.

Off camera there is the sound of crying from the adults in the room. It's an intense moment of pure, unscripted, unconditional love.

After wiping his tears and composing himself, Curtis turns his head to his right, unable to see, but with the perfect vision of his heart he begins waving excitedly at his little brother.

Who sheepishly waves back.

The two continue waving at each other until Curtis reaches out, grabs his brother by the neck, pulls him in close, and cuddles him tightly for ten seconds. Finally, Curtis kisses his brother's head and exhales deeply, as if to say, *Okay, that's what I needed. Let's do this.*

I've watched the video dozens of times. I cry every time. Because I see a little boy coming back to life through the presence and touch of his siblings.

A couple of weeks later, Brad sent me another video. This one was of Curtis sitting up, trying to tie his shoes. Stunningly, his eyesight had returned.

Not long after, Brad forwarded another video. Of Curtis speaking to his mom. His ability to talk had returned.

The last video he sent shows Curtis and his little brother playing catch in the backyard of their home in Louisiana.

Adrienne got her wish. Curtis came home.

How could this have happened? The medical community at Memorial can't explain it.

The skeptics may call it simply good luck. Cynics might say Curtis wasn't that seriously injured.

After I chatted with his parents, we agreed: we believe it's the healing power of God's love.

And sometimes that profound healing occurs through the contagion of joy, through the innocent, accepting, life-affirming touch of others.

We were not made to go through life alone.

We need to remember the curative power of a cuddle, and the amazing effects it can have on our body and our psyche.

We need to remember the power of a simple high five to elevate play and encourage greatness.

We need to recall the power of a hug to help us share our burdens and remember that we're not alone, that we belong.

Most of us commute to work in our cars, alone, or plug into our devices on public transportation. When we wave to acquaintances or chat amiably with the cashier, it's often at a surface level.

It's time to dig deep, my friend. We let ourselves be ignored, but we long to be seen.

We desire to be heard.

We want to be known.

We pray to be loved.

We want to belong.

Without true connection, we will wither away.

With it, we survive, sustain, and thrive, together.

23

A Piece of the Puzzle

"Mr. O'Leary, can I talk to you for a moment?"

When I hear "Mr." in front of my name, I usually glance around the room for my dad. Although I'm happily progressing into my forties, I much prefer to be called John.

In particular, I don't like hearing the words "Mr. O'Leary, can I talk to you for a moment?" when I am picking up my kids from school. Especially when they come from Henry's teacher.

Henry is number three in our family, the youngest of my boys. He is incredibly fun, funny, outgoing, athletic, and bright. He loves music, laughing, animals, roughhousing, and Fortnite. He is always moving, always dancing, and always smiling. He's an amazing kid.

All this passionate exuberance for life means that in addition to bringing great joy to his friends and family, he can occasionally be a handful in class. In today's season of politically correct jargon he might be considered a bit "spirited" or "active."

I looked compassionately at this wonderful teacher, imagining the unique challenges of educating my son, as well as the children of two dozen other parents. So when she asked to talk, I was bracing for the worst.

"Henry was a little disruptive in class today. I warned him several times to stop talking. I tried several times to redirect him. And eventually I called him to my desk in order to give him one final warning." Oh boy, here goes, I thought, bracing for the worst.

She put her right hand on my shoulder, squared me up as if to ensure I was still following along with her, and continued.

"I was getting impatient. I had already moved him to two different work groups and neither led to success. So I told him, 'Take a good look around the room and find one group where you don't have friends who will distract you from your work.'"

The teacher paused, seeming to be stifling a laugh.

"I watched as Henry stood and stared out at his classroom. Finally, he looked back at me, and said, 'But it's just so hard!'

"'Why is it so hard, Henry?' I asked with frustration.

"'Because everywhere I look, all I see are friends.'"

The teacher wore a look of pride as she finished Henry's sentence. She went on to tell me, "I think Henry already knows one of the most important lessons out there: that the world is filled with potential friends. When you chat with him on the way home, please tell him thanks for reminding his teacher today of that important lesson. I needed it."

Everywhere I look, all I see are friends!

Wise words from a child. How many of *us* could say them?

Is that how you feel as you look around *your* classroom? Be honest.

How about when you walk into the office or grocery store?

Do you feel that way waiting at the train station, or going through TSA security lines, or gazing at fellow commuters on your drive home?

Sadly, we do not live in a society that sees friends everywhere. Indeed, as you may have already suspected, we've never felt more alone.

Cigna recently released research on what they call "the epidemic of loneliness" facing our society. Despite the "connectedness" of our generation and our ability to reach one another anywhere at any time via our devices, we aren't truly connecting. Though we spend up to three hours on our phone each day, that isn't the kind of connection we crave. Researchers have determined that people are happiest on the days when they socialize between five and six hours.

But we, on average, socialize just forty-one minutes a day.[1]

Only forty-one minutes a day spending time with friends, family, and loved ones?

No wonder we feel alone.

Even when we are with people, we sometimes fall into "phubbing," or snubbing the person physically in front of us to tend to the urgency of our phones.

This loneliness, this isolation, this emptiness in our hearts is not only devastating to us, it is killing us.

Unfortunately, I'm not being overly dramatic.

It is one of the reasons more than 1.5 million people attempt suicide in the United States each year. Yes, 1.5 million people a year in America reach a point in their lives where they feel there is no room for hope, no reason to continue. It's an epidemic that claimed the lives of more than fifty thousand people last year. Fifty thousand moms, dads, sisters, brothers, children, and friends. Gone forever.

My friend, there are plenty of good people trying to turn the tide. Trying to raise awareness of mental health issues and remove the stigma associated with them so more people can ask for help. Trying to create government programs so we can provide more resources to the populations that need them most.

I'm not a psychologist or a doctor or a community organizer. But I do know that there is one thing we could do to help address this pervasive loneliness.

We can put down our phones and reach out to someone.

We can let down our guard and share the problems that we are facing.

We can let people into our struggles and joys, our ups and our downs, while listening to and accepting them in theirs, and get back to the life-giving experience of living life together.

Fitting In

Amy Crawford is a fifth-grade teacher.

She has been serving children in Knoxville, Tennessee, for more than thirty years. Teaching is a demanding profession. Our teachers are underpaid, overworked, and far too often underappreciated. They instruct and elevate our children academically. The even more important work is instilling and fostering skills that will allow our children to be kind, resilient, respectful citizens of this world. It's mission work. It shapes society. It changes the world, one lesson, one class, one life at a time.

Sometimes the work can be challenging and the rewards hard to see.

But early in Amy's career, she saw firsthand how important her job was.

There was a boy in her class who was often disengaged. He was rude to others, and indifferent to her efforts to bring him out of his shell. He turned assignments in late. He was disrespectful. In short, he was the kind of kid who is easy to give up on. After all, if someone isn't even willing to try, why should we put forth all the effort?

One day while Amy was cleaning up papers around his desk, she found a poem he'd written. Reading the poem changed her life.

And, in time, his.

Amy is a dear friend and shared this poem with me recently; the author has allowed it to be shared in this book. It is a powerful piece of writing that shows how deeply we can feel out of place, even at a very young age.

I AM THE PIECE THAT NEVER FITS

I am the piece that never fits
I wonder why people hate me for who I am
I hear the cry of loneliness that comes from me
I see my sad, strange, different self in the mirror
I want someone on my side

I am the piece that never fits.
I pretend that words can never hurt me
I feel the urge to run away from myself
I touch the wet tear from my eye rolling down my face
I worry my future will be me, myself, and I
I cry because I am the cheese; everyone is the mouse
I am the piece that never fits

I understand that no one likes me
I say that there is no place for people like me in the world
I dream of a place where I actually fit in
I try to make new friends,
And I hope to, but still
I am the piece that never fits.

As Amy held this piece of paper in her hands and read the heartfelt message it shared, she was overcome by emotion. She was not just struck by how sad and alone this child felt, but stunned that she had missed the depth of his suffering, despite the fact that he sat directly in front of her in her classroom. Not only that, but she hadn't realized that in her midst was an incredibly gifted writer, a student with deep feelings and a precise way of putting them into words.

She walked into school the next day with a new passion to show this child that he had a place in her classroom. She spent every day of the rest of that school year seeking to become a friend to a young boy who felt he had no one. She encouraged the boy who felt he didn't fit in to realize the beauty of all of our jagged edges.

In time, with love and with focus, by being surrounded by supportive students and introduced to new mentors, the author of the poem began to see that he did have friends, he was a gift, and he did fit in.

Today he's a college graduate, gainfully employed, happily married, and passionate about life. He stays in touch with Amy, the teacher he credits with showing him that all was not lost.

Many times in my life I, too, have felt as if I am the piece that doesn't fit.

The kid on the end of the bench, not able to participate in the game.

The adolescent without a date.

The man who puts himself out there publicly—and frequently deals with isolating stares that come with that exposure.

But of course, it's not just me.

Many of us feel as if we do not fit in.

And when we feel like we don't fit in, we feel alone.

Did you know that loneliness is as harmful to your well-being as smoking cigarettes?[2] It's as destructive as smoking fifteen cigarettes a day.

But we don't see the surgeon general's warnings on our loneliness, our isolation, and our sadness. We should.

Here's the truth. We are not alone. In our enormous human family, there is no such thing as an individual who has no value. There is no such thing as a piece that doesn't fit.

When we insist on standing off to the side, isolated, we may feel like a jagged piece, and it is hard to accept that we belong.

But when we are joined to the whole, we see that together, we create a beautiful masterpiece.

Our jagged pieces are perfect. They have purpose. They are our power.

We aren't meant to go through life on our own.

Our edges may be rough and ragged and scarred. But we do fit. Perfectly imperfect into the massive mosaic of life.

Let me show you how.

24

Stop Hiding in the Shadows

"EXCUSE ME," COUGHED A CRICKET WHO'D SEEN GERALD
EARLIER ON. "BUT SOMETIMES WHEN YOU'RE DIFFERENT,
YOU JUST NEED A DIFFERENT SONG."

Giles Andreae, *Giraffes Can't Dance*

The kids were loving it. Their eyes were open wide and their heads were bobbing along to the beat of the music.

I didn't blame them. It was a great movie.

The Greatest Showman is the Hollywood version of the life of P. T. Barnum.

And by Hollywood version, I mean that they probably took some liberties with the narrative. They may have made Barnum a bit more handsome than he truly was. They may have beefed up some of the drama, and sugarcoated some of the pain. But the essence of who P. T. Barnum was and what he did remains the same. The founder of the famous Barnum & Bailey Circus, Barnum searched far and wide for the most peculiar individuals alive to attract people to his show. Utilizing individuals from various ethnic backgrounds, with unique talents, and with wildly different looks, in order to drive large audiences to a celebration of spectacle, he employed a seven-foot giant; a man who was only three feet tall; a seven-hundred-pound man; conjoined twins.

Individually, they were castoffs, unwanted, ignored, pitied, or even despised.

But when brought together, they became something else.

Something to celebrate.

In order to take center stage, though, these characters needed to recognize that what seemed to be their greatest imperfection was in fact their greatest asset.

The very thing they had been hiding for years needed to come out into the light.

When Lettie Lutz (played by Keala Settle) stepped to the center of the ring to sing "This Is Me," she sang what became an anthem for anyone who had ever felt a bit out of place.

Lettie was a fully bearded lady, an anomaly. She had spent most of her life hiding from the gaze of strangers. But P. T. Barnum gave her permission to step out, and step into her power.

"I am not a stranger to the dark," she began.

Barnum's entire cast was once sheltered from stares and hidden from view to save them from ridicule and insults. No one wanted their broken parts.

But when the impresario invited them out of the shadows, it did something powerful. It allowed them to own their differentness, to celebrate their scars.

Joining a band of misfits allowed Lettie to embrace who she was, flaws and all.

This shift was powerful.

She finished her anthem with these words:

I'm not scared to be seen.
I make no apologies . . .
This is me!

I'm not scared to be seen.

These words reveal what is often holding us back from true connection with others.

We are afraid to be seen.

Sure, we curate an image of ourselves on the Internet, but we hide away the real us. We don't own our broken parts. We don't share our deepest burdens.

We turn away from connection because we think we have something to hide. After all, what if we get too close? What if they see the truth? Better to stand apart, alone, protected from view.

But there is great power, my friend, in stepping into the light.

There is immense healing in sharing scars, exposing weaknesses, and revealing shame.

It is the only way we'll let people in.

We Are the Same

Even after a speaking career that spans more than a decade and the positive reception to my first book, *On Fire,* I still feel anxiety about showing people my scars—the ones on the outside, and the ones on the inside.

Perhaps nowhere does that fear manifest itself more acutely than when I speak to Focus Marines.

Focus Marines was established a decade ago, when a group of Marines began seeing a significant uptick in both PTSD in returning servicemembers and a lack of services to support them once they were home. They funded an outreach program for veterans with PTSD to receive eight days of counseling, leadership training, anger management, and professional development. I've been fortunate to partner with them more than forty times over the past decade. Each time I feel as if I stand on sacred ground when I walk into the room.

And for many of those sessions I felt as if I didn't really belong.

They fought and served on the front lines of war for our country. I haven't.

They earned the right to wear a uniform, to salute our flag, and to be honored by others.

I have not.

They are muscular, they're chiseled, they're warriors.

Um, have you seen me?

One of the ways I used to armor up, to try to make myself feel worthy, was by wearing an oversized sport coat so that I had more physical stature when I entered the room. It was an attempt to cover up my weaknesses, to look bigger than I was. It also conveniently covered the scars on my arms that are immediately apparent when I don't wear long sleeves. This was my uniform, my way of fitting in for the first nine years I spoke at Focus Marines.

This whole trying-to-be-something-I'm-not? Trying to fit in, belong, and feel worthy? It's something I've been doing for years.

It's what I did in grade school through the use of humor. My being the class clown distracted everyone from thinking about the kid who got burned.

It's what I did in high school and college with drinking. Being the life of the party made me feel more comfortable, helped me imagine I was fitting in.

It's what I did in my adult life with performance. Being an entrepreneur, running a business, being successful made me feel worthy.

Throughout it all, though, I hid away the broken parts.

A few years ago, a chance encounter with a young man after a speaking engagement helped change that. I had finished speaking at a camp and was standing in line at the dining hall when I felt a tug on my jacket sleeve.

Looking down, I saw a little boy with a transcendent smile.

He looked up at me and said, "We are the same."

I knelt to his level, looked into his eyes, and responded playfully, "We are?"

He nodded and repeated himself: "We are the same!"

He then held up his right hand and revealed that, like me, he didn't have any fingers on it. He came closer, gave me a hug, introduced himself as Caleb. And one more time he said, "We are the same."

He was no more than nine years old. I was approaching forty.

He was African American. My ancestors came from southern Ireland.

He was born in an urban environment and had limited resources. I was born in the Midwest and into a life of privilege.

He was wearing a T-shirt and a pair of athletic shorts, ready for a day of summer-camp fun. I was wearing a dark suit, a long-sleeved shirt, and dress shoes, totally overdressed for the day.

And yet, looking into his eyes, seeing his joy, observing his hand—and his heart—I realized he saw what many of us too frequently miss.

The very things we feel make us undesirable, or different, or broken, are in reality the very things that pull us closest together. They are the things that remind us of our shared stories and the larger truth that we're not alone.

With Caleb's example and encouragement, I shed that suit jacket—not only for the rest of that day at summer camp, but for my first speech the following week.

It was a Monday evening, and the audience happened to be a bunch of Marines. I showed up that evening without a suit coat or long sleeves. I came in wearing short sleeves, exposing skinny arms, scarred skin, no fingers. I put it all out there.

No more hiding.

My anxiety was high as the leader introduced me, but I tried to remember Caleb's wise words. *We are the same.* Though I felt out of my league with the men and women in that room, they too knew what it was to embark on a challenging journey when the outcome is unclear.

They too knew what it felt like to face injury, and recovery, and a life that had completely changed . . . but still held possibility.

They too had fought some terrible battles and accumulated thick scars—some on the outside—all on the inside.

We are the same.

As I approached the stage, as I stood before them and prepared to speak, something happened that had never happened before in my entire career: I received a standing ovation . . . before uttering a word.

As I stood before them, scars and all, rather than viewing me as different, less than, or inferior, they saw a guy they could relate to, who might actually understand their journey.

Owning my inadequacies had allowed the walls to come down and the connection to begin. All without saying a word.

I'm not scared to be seen.

I make no apologies.

This is me.

When we are honest about who we are, embrace it, and share it with others, that's when true connection occurs. When hearts open. When walls come down.

I spoke with Brené Brown about leadership on my podcast. She shared something that has stuck with me, advice I've attempted to heed: "Fear is not the barrier to courageous leadership. The biggest barrier is self-protection. The way we armor up. You can't lead from an armored place."[1]

I learned firsthand that day how powerful it is to take the armor off. My goal is to never put it back on.

My friend, what is your armor? What's that barrier you've established to keep others from knowing the real you? How is that affecting the way you show up, the way you connect, the way you lead?

It is time to let our guard down and step into the light. It is time to own our scars, our stories, our weaknesses, and our wounds so that we can get back to celebrating who we are and connecting with those around us.

We are the same. We belong.

And we are worthy of celebration. Exactly as we are.

25

Join the Party

[PEOPLE] FORGET THAT THEY TOO WOULD SEEM DIFFERENT IF THEY COULD ONLY SEE THEMSELVES THROUGH OTHER PEOPLE'S EYES. . . . BUT IMAGINE HOW DREADFULLY DULL THIS WORLD OF OURS WOULD BE IF EVERYBODY WOULD LOOK, THINK, EAT, DRESS, AND ACT THE SAME!

Peter Spier, *People*

After I finished speaking to a group of financial advisors, a gentleman approached, thanked me for my story, shared a bit of his, and then told me he wanted to introduce me to a special family. He told me I'd love Amy and Ben, their kids, and their unbelievable story.

He was right.

Amy and Ben Wright were a couple in love.

They enjoyed meaningful work and two healthy children. As good as things were, their joy expanded with excitement about their third pregnancy.

But the pregnancy was more difficult than they anticipated, and their son Beau's arrival didn't go exactly as planned.

When the nurses placed Beau in Amy's arms, the doctor came alongside with a warning. There were some indicators that Beau might have Down syndrome. The doctors weren't sure and planned to do some tests. They would know in a few days.

Three days later, the diagnosis was confirmed.

Amy and Ben wept; they didn't know exactly what this would mean. But they knew their lives had changed. They wondered: How would Beau learn to walk? Talk? Would he ever go to school? Get married?

Sympathetic encouragement arrived in the form of flowers, cards, and meals. One well-intentioned neighbor brought Amy dinner, gave her a mighty hug, and began to share how deeply sorry she was. The neighbor tried to offer encouragement, but was simply unable to. The sadness was just too great.

People treated this diagnosis like a funeral.

While it was certainly a disruption to their perfectly ordered life, Amy and Ben eventually accepted the news, embracing their son and the love he exuded. They knew the typical trajectory of parenthood would be altered. But they were ready to experience all the joy and beauty Beau would bring.

While raising Beau was not as easy as raising their older children, Ben and Amy realized quickly that, far from being a burden, Beau's Down syndrome was an unexpected, delightful gift.

Beau exuded curiosity, a contagious enthusiasm for life, and a persistent joy, seen not just in his smile, but in his sparkling eyes. He taught them to not take things so seriously, to always find occasion to laugh; he revealed how easy it is to connect with others. Beau tended to embrace every person they encountered. While it took some getting used to, and a few explanations, it also provided countless opportunities to make new friends. All thanks to their incredible son.

As Beau grew, his parents received another unexpected gift: Amy was pregnant with their fourth child. Because of certain risk factors in the pregnancy they ran a battery of tests.

Amy remembers exactly where she was when her phone rang again. The physician spoke slowly, solemnly, reminding Amy that because of Beau, there were inherent risks with another pregnancy.

The little girl she was carrying had a condition called cystic fibroma. There was only a 25-percent chance that Amy would be able to carry this pregnancy to term. After a long pause, the physician added that there might be some chromosomal abnormalities as well, an indicator of Down syndrome.

At this point, Amy was focused on bringing her baby safely into the world. She wasn't worried about possible abnormalities. She just wanted her baby to arrive safely, to have a chance at life, no matter what that looked like.

As they began to monitor her condition, the doctors kept Amy and Ben abreast of her daughter's health. A second phone call confirmed that this little girl also had Down syndrome.

As the couple hung up the phone, Amy and Ben looked at each other and wept—but this time from joy, not from sadness.

Yes, they were aware that children with Down syndrome faced medical challenges. Yes, they knew that the trajectory of their child's life would look a bit different.

But they had redefined perfection.

Perfection was neither looking like everyone else, nor competing with others on their scale of success.

Perfection was embracing each child wholly for how they actually were.

Beau had taught them things they'd learned from no one else in their lives. And when, a few months later, their little girl was safely placed in Amy's arms, they were grateful for her health. And they knew she was perfect.

Thomas Merton, the celebrated monk and author, said, "The beginning of this love is the will to let those we love be perfectly themselves, the resolution not to twist them to fit our own image."[1]

Is that how you love your partner or spouse?

Is that how you love your parents, in-laws, neighbors, friends, and colleagues? Is it how you approach people from different ethnic backgrounds, political affiliations, religious beliefs? With a devout willingness, a resolution, to accept them perfectly as they are, not as you would have them?

Amy and Ben learned how to love their two youngest children for who they were. No molding or twisting to fit something they were not. But open to all that was different in them, and the beauty that came with it.

"We fear what we don't understand," they now say. "We fear what we don't have experience with. We fear what we don't know. And when you don't know anything about—in this case—Down syndrome, there's a lot of fear; there is judgment and preconceived notions about it. We had been through all of that. We knew we were going to win the lottery. Twice."[2]

We are very good at making snap judgments. But often those judgments are wrong. And because of fear, we don't step close enough to have those misconceptions corrected.

Amy and Ben want to alter the idea that we should feel sorry for people with disabilities. Amy and Ben know that this perception is wrong.

One out of four people will experience a disability at some point in their lives. If we can learn to recognize that those disabilities make us not less human but even *more* human, we can stop avoiding these people and instead celebrate them.

Amy and Ben have begun to do just that. As their two little ones grow older, Amy and Ben have become aware of just how few employment opportunities people with disabilities are afforded as adults. Eighty percent of adults with intellectual or developmental delays are unemployed.[3] Yet Amy and Ben knew just how capable their children were.

So in 2016, Amy and Ben opened Bitty & Beau's Coffee, a community coffee shop that employs people with IDD (intellectual or developmental disabilities). They *intentionally* hire individuals with special needs.

They do this not just to provide opportunities for employment, but also to create a community that doesn't merely allow that some people are made differently, but that *celebrates* it. "Bitty & Beau's Coffee is a new lens, one that changes the way people see other people. It's about human value. It's about acceptance. It's about inclusion."[4]

Although their business strategist suggested they add a drive-through window, making it easier for patrons to grab their coffee on the go, Amy and Ben wanted instead to create a space where customers not only received a great cup of coffee, but found an engaging, welcoming community in which to enjoy it. When people walk into Bitty & Beau's, they see people pulling up chairs and having conversations that matter. Patrons get to know the staff, deepening their understanding of just how much people with IDD have to share and that there is nothing to fear.

"My employees are not broken," says Amy. "The 200 million people living with an IDD are not broken. What is broken is the lens through which we view people with disabilities."[5]

Our idea of success is often built on what people think of us. Part of the pain of having a child with a disability stems from how he or she is compared with other people. Amy and Ben know that loving what you have instead of worrying about how other people are going to judge you can allow you to embrace the disruptions in your life. And to recognize that those disruptions can truly bring blessings.

Open Your Eyes

One of Amy and Ben's employees is Elizabeth, a woman with Down syndrome. She takes orders with passion, conviction, and joy.

Recently, a young couple came in. When Elizabeth noticed that the woman was expecting, she walked out from behind the counter, gave her a hug, and congratulated the couple on the baby before going back to work.

About an hour later the couple came back to the counter. The gentleman stood back a few steps as the expectant mother asked to speak to Elizabeth. She explained that this was their first child.

"Our baby," she said softly, trying to keep her composure, almost whispering so as to not let the world know the difficult secret she was bearing, "has Down syndrome, too."

There was a momentary pause as Elizabeth considered the news.

Her face then lit up. As she pumped her fist in the air, she screamed a single word: "Yes!" She rushed from behind the counter and gave both parents a mighty hug.

Then she raised her voice and announced, "Everyone, I need your attention."

The bustling coffee shop quieted.

With all eyes fixed on her, Elizabeth made an announcement: "These two people are expecting a baby. Their first baby. And the baby is going to have Down syndrome." She pumped her fist into the air again and excitedly yelled, *"Yes!"*

The coffee shop erupted into applause. And the young couple dissolved into tears.

They had just discovered a place where they belonged.

Amy and Ben Wright opened Bitty & Beau's Coffee shop in the hopes of changing the world. It's working, in their community of Wilmington, North Carolina. But it is being noticed far beyond that.

Amy Wright received the CNN 2017 Hero of the Year award. In her acceptance speech, broadcast nationally, Amy concluded her remarks by turning away from the live audience and looking directly into the cameras. Knowing her two youngest were watching and up past their bedtime, she closed with these words: "Bitty and Beau, I know you are home watching this. I need you to know that you are perfect. I would not change either of you for the world. But I would change the world for you."[6]

My friend, the world needs to change. We need to stop seeing differences as something to avoid, and instead see them as something that brings us together. That we all belong.

In our attempts to protect our children, we inadvertently signal that the unknown is scary. We teach them, "Don't talk to strangers, don't talk about differences, and don't stare!" But inherent in those statements is the idea that other people aren't to be trusted, that different is bad, and that wanting to understand is a mistake. It creates in their impressionable eyes a lens of *us versus them*. And once that lens is in place, it is very hard to remove.

We teach them to turn away from those who look different from us, rather than allowing their curiosity to remind us that differences can be invitations to connect, inquire, and learn.

The World Happiness Report considers trust to be one of the six factors that lead to happiness. "A successful society is one in which people have a high level of trust in each other—including family members, colleagues, friends, strangers, and institutions such as government. Social trust spurs a sense of life satisfaction."[7]

Can you claim that factor in our current society? More personally, can you claim it in your office, your school, your community? Heck, can you even claim it in your social media feed? A collection of individuals, striving together with a high level of openness to differing opinions and trust in one another?

Few of us could.

All of us should.

When we teach children to be wary of those they don't know and situations that are different, we shut down the inherent sense of belonging that once helped them to connect with one another and celebrate what it means to be a part of the human family.

We forget that we are all the same. That all lives are sacred.

That we can walk into a room and see it as filled not with strangers to be feared but with potential friends.

There is no piece that doesn't fit.

We *all* belong, and we are all worthy of celebration.

Let's stop standing off in isolation.

Let's stop pretending to be who we're not. And let's instead pull up a chair, sit down with a cup of coffee, and celebrate how great it is to have the chance to go through life—together.

26

You Belong

IT IS WHEN WE ARE MOST LOST THAT WE SOMETIMES FIND
OUR TRUEST FRIENDS.

**Cynthia Rylant, *Walt Disney's Snow White
and the Seven Dwarfs***

I was more nervous than usual.

I was visiting a relatively small school called Catholic High in a relatively small town in Louisiana called New Iberia.

I'd been invited to deliver a message of setting big goals, connecting with a higher calling, being bold in faith, and radically accepting of others. But there was a surprise planned for the end of my speech that I was even more excited about.

The gymnasium was packed with hundreds of students. From fourth-grade students on my right, all the way around to seniors on my left, the bleachers were filled. Seated in foldout chairs on the floor were administrators, parents, and guests from the community.

I shared my story of getting burned as a kid, and spoke of all the individuals who stepped forward to make a difference for me. Then I displayed a picture of what I looked like before I returned to elementary school on the screen behind me. White bandages covered an area on my scalp that had just been used for the thirteenth time as a skin graft donor site. I was seated in a wheelchair. My hands rested on my lap, revealing the effects of the amputation of my fingers.

I then asked the students gathered around me: "Now, if you looked like that, would you be nervous about going back to school?"

The loud rumble throughout the auditorium confirmed that yes, they would be.

"Why?" I asked.

One of the children in the first row frantically waved her hand. (It's always the youngest who raise their hands first!) After I called on her, she offered, "Because you look so different. Maybe you worried the older kids were going to make fun of you."

"That's an awesome answer, and you're exactly right! That's exactly what I had been afraid of."

I then shared the story of what had actually happened when I returned to my school, after being absent for fourteen months.

I left school on a Friday afternoon in January, an athletic, popular fourth-grade boy. I was returning more than a year later, on a March morning, as a fifth grader. I'd missed a lot. But more than that, I was returning in a wheelchair, without my fingers, scarred, scared, and unsure of what school would be like. Would I still have any friends? Would I be able to get from class to class? How would I get my books from my backpack to my locker? Would the teachers treat me differently?

Deep down, I was worried: Would I still belong?

After an early-morning physical therapy appointment, Mom drove me in our old Mercury station wagon. Leaning back against the red vinyl seat, I sat quietly next to her, terrified about the day ahead of me.

I'd never been wild about going to school. Even before being burned, I had welcomed any excuse to miss school and stay home.

Snow day? Check.

Water-main break at school? Check.

National or religious holiday? Check.

Illness? Check.

Potential illness? Check!

On that March day, I took a deep breath. The school was around the corner. Could I come up with an excuse to postpone my return?

But it was too late. She'd made the turn, and school was within sight.

But then I heard shouts and screams, and I looked up.

Hundreds of students lined both sides of the streets.

Mom slowed down the station wagon, and we crawled toward the school. As we did, kids on both sides of the road were shouting welcomes, waving signs, smiling excitedly at me. They were trying to make the little boy who felt he didn't belong, who was sure he was a piece that just didn't fit, feel welcomed back. Feel that he belonged, and that he fit perfectly.

As we rolled into the parking lot and Mom stopped the car, the cheering got louder. Mom got out, opened my door, and helped me out. Being a cool fifth grader, I'm not sure I even looked up or waved to acknowledge the cheers. But I heard them. I was profoundly moved by them. I will never forget them, as long as I live.

As our principal propped open the door into the school, I saw that my classmates lined both sides of the hallway. These were kids I'd spent five years getting to know, many of whom I hadn't seen in more than a year.

As I rolled through the welcoming tunnel that they'd formed, tears sprung from my eyes—tears of happiness. I felt embraced, enveloped by love.

Maybe, just maybe, everything was going to be okay.

The welcome didn't end with that carefully orchestrated morning. It lasted all year as I carefully navigated my new reality. My classmates didn't look away. They didn't avoid me. The other kids didn't mock me; they engaged with me. They said hello. They helped me with my books. They *fought* over who got to push my wheelchair.

I was burned, scarred, broken, and different.

But I was back.

And they let me know it was okay. That I still fit.

Time to Smile

Sawabona.

This is the traditional greeting for tribes in northern Natal in South Africa. Anytime they see a friend, family member, visitor, or stranger, they welcome that person with the word *sawabona.*

The friend, family member, visitor, or stranger then replies with *sikhona.*

Sawabona translates as "I see you."

And *sikhona* means "I'm here."

I love that greeting. To me, that is the heart of connection. Looking at each other fully. Not turning away. Not ignoring or judging. Not holding back or hiding.

I see you.

I'm here.

With those words, you immediately feel embraced, welcomed, accepted. What a difference such a greeting might make for us all.

On that first day as a fifth grader, when I was wildly apprehensive about going back to school, those kids, their waves, their smiles, their handheld posters, their encouragement, let me know that I was seen. That they were here for me.

It was a beautiful gift. And I hoped to give it to someone else today.

As I finished my story in that school in New Iberia, I asked the students gathered around me to imagine how that kind of welcome on my first day back at school had made me feel.

The words *good, great, awesome,* and *loved* echoed out from the bleachers.

"So," I continued, "how would you like the chance to make someone else feel that welcome?"

The crowd roared excitedly.

"Let me tell you a story," I said. "About a year ago, I met a second-grade boy in the hospital. He was in a terrible car accident and had to be airlifted far away from home, all the way to a hospital in Jackson,

Mississippi. The boy's family was told that he wasn't expected to live. And that if he did survive, he would never be able to see, or speak, again. He'd certainly never return to school."

I paused.

"Well, that young man defied those dire prognoses."

The crowd cheered.

"Eventually he returned to his elementary school. He is now in third grade. And this brave young man is considering attending school here next year."

There was another roar of excitement.

"He wanted to visit today to see if he might fit in."

The room buzzed with energy.

"In a moment, I'm going to ask him to stand," I said, "but I want you to make sure he knows that you see him, that he fits in here, and that he belongs in this community."

With that I said, "Curtis, would you stand and wave to your future classmates?"

A blond boy with dark-rimmed glasses stood up from a chair on the gymnasium floor. He looked down briefly before looking up and waving sheepishly to the six hundred kids lining the bleachers.

As he did, those students leapt from their seats, shouting encouragement and offering a prolonged standing ovation of welcome. As the applause rained down, Curtis made his way to me, and he gave me a hug and a fist bump.

After the two-minute ovation finally quieted down, he gave me something his parents had never thought they'd see in that ICU more than a year earlier: an enormous smile.

Curtis was home.

My friend, *you belong here.* You are worthy. You are enough. And we celebrate you.

Your assignment is to remind those you encounter of that same truth in their lives.

We belong.

We are each an essential piece of the puzzle.

Let's remember how beautiful it is to do life together. No, we don't all look the same. We don't all vote the same way. We don't all worship at the same church or mosque or synagogue. We don't even always get along.

But we belong.

Let's stop putting up walls and building fences. Instead, let's take them down. Let's put aside our masks. Let's open up our lives, not only by how we accept others, but by embracing who we are.

Let's remove the bondage of isolation and lift the veil of perceived unworthiness.

I believe it will empower us to do great things—together.

Sense #4: Belonging

I am the piece that never fits.
Or
I belong. Just as I am.

My friend, I don't know what you've been told.
I don't know how you feel, what scars you bear physically
or which ones lie hidden deep within your heart.
But I know one thing.
You are beautifully, wondrously made.
You have within you gifts to share with the world.
You were put here on this earth for a reason.
We all are.

No matter our skin color, nationality, economic situation, or
personal beliefs and values.
We come from one tribe. We fit together.
And we need one another.
The epidemic of loneliness can be cured.
It's time to tear down our fences and start to celebrate.
All are invited.
But first you've got to show up.

Step out of the shadows.
Embrace your intrinsic value.
And share who you are.
Doing so will empower you to lift your voice
and proudly sing, *This is me.*
And then join the parade.
When we come together, we can truly change the world.

Freedom

Stepping Off the Sideline
and Getting Back in the Game

NEVER DO ANYTHING BY HALVES IF YOU WANT
TO GET AWAY WITH IT. BE OUTRAGEOUS.
GO THE WHOLE HOG. MAKE SURE EVERYTHING
YOU DO IS SO COMPLETELY CRAZY IT'S UNBELIEVABLE.

Roald Dahl, *Matilda*

freedom:

(V) TO OWN YOUR CHOICES, CLAIM YOUR
POWER, DARE BOLDLY, AND GIVE LIFE YOUR ALL

27

Play to Win

MOTHERS FOR MILES AROUND WORRIED ABOUT ZUCKERMAN'S SWING. THEY FEARED SOME CHILD WOULD FALL OFF. BUT NO CHILD EVER DID. CHILDREN ALMOST ALWAYS HANG ON TO THINGS TIGHTER THAN THEIR PARENTS THINK THEY WILL.

E. B. White, *Charlotte's Web*

There's no time of the year I love more than summer vacation with my family.

We stay in an old beach town in Florida right on the Gulf. We leave behind our laptops, smartphones, dress shoes, and responsibilities. We shed our watches, stop racing around, and don't take work calls.

Mornings are spent under an umbrella on the beach, building sandcastles, or taking walks. Afternoons are for hammocks, bike rides, or reading. And after dinner, we usually play a game. Sorry. Risk. Monopoly. Sometimes even heated rounds of poker.

Several years ago my oldest son, Jack, and I were engrossed in a game of Texas Hold'em. And let me tell you, this kid goes all in on just about every hand. When I call him on it, he has good cards. When I don't, turns out he is bluffing. This perfect storm of me being a terrible poker player, Jack having Lady Luck on his side and his boldness of play, means I lose almost every hand.

To add salt to the wound, he handles winning with the subtle grace and humility of a high school marching band.

After one such victory and the raucous celebration that followed,

I asked Jack with an exasperated smile, "Dude, how are you totally destroying me in these games?"

Jack, shuffling the deck in preparation for his next conquest, glanced up and said, "Dad, you play not to lose." He then looked down at the cards, focusing on the important work at hand, before adding, "I play to win."

His words struck something deep inside me.

Jack was right. I was playing not to lose. And not just in poker. In life as well.

As I watched him shuffle the cards behind the stack of his winnings, I thought about how differently I lead my life today than I did when I was his age.

Instead of jumping out of my seat to be the first one chosen, I sit back, play it cool, and pretend I don't care.

Rather than be the first to raise my hand, I wait for someone else to act, to fix, to solve, to speak up.

Rather than take a risk, I'd prefer to play it safe. I don't want to draw attention to myself.

Think about it. When was the last time you felt like you were playing to win? I don't mean when was the last time you won a game, scored a goal, earned a promotion, or beat some kid at a game of poker. I mean when was the last time you risked failure, gave it your all, and stepped in to participate fully in every area of your life? When was the last time you felt totally and wholly alive, like you left nothing on the table?

As Jack gathered yet another round of winnings, I realized that my kids were not shackled by the fear that dominated my adult mindset.

They weren't afraid to look silly.

They had no reservations whatsoever about getting naked, singing loudly, asking questions, or trying something new.

They're free.

Free to try.

Free to laugh.

Free to engage.

Free to fail.

Free to rise back up.

Free to win.

We are born free. Inherent within each of us is the ability to get back to that state: to dare greatly, go big, and run forward unhindered by expectations, judgment, and fear.

Let's be clear. Freedom does not mean lack of responsibility. It does not mean you get to live as if you're at Woodstock every day. Far from it.

Freedom necessitates owning the power and responsibility of choice. It means you hold the reins, you determine the course, and you certainly own your perspective. Instead of having a master or a past to blame, you're empowered to make choices and determine your future. It is the very opposite of slavery.

But over time, we lose touch with our sense of freedom. We feel caged in by expectations, burdened by responsibilities, shackled by fear. We forget that we are free to get in the game. That life is waiting for us to step up to the plate and take a mighty swing.

Too often we remain in the dugout. And in doing so we become spectators. We shrug and complain about the game, but we don't participate in making it right. We stop stepping up. We stop stepping in. We worry we might strike out.

But failure isn't something to be avoided. It is essential for our development.

Psychologists today are increasingly concerned about the next generation of children who have been raised to play it safe and be careful.

"Helicopter parenting" is a term coined in 1969 by Dr. Haim Ginott. It refers to a style of parenting in which the parents tend to hover, to be a bit overbearing, ever watchful, and overprotective. Today the epidemic of overprotective parents has spread beyond helicopter parents to bulldozing parents. These parents don't hover; they take things into their own hands. Any risks, adversity, and roadblocks that might hinder success for their children are forcefully pushed out of the way. This kind of parenting hurts our adolescents as we try to build the best future for them. But it also adversely impacts our little ones.

Risk-taking is an essential component of play in early childhood. It is how children learn to regulate fear and anger. As kids climb higher up the tree or shimmy up the pole, they are testing their limits; they are assessing what they can handle. "Interfering with risk-taking mammalian play imperils our young by undermining their confidence," journalist Leslie Kendall Dye writes.[1] She had a daughter who was a daredevil and who constantly wanted to find ways to test how strong she was. Bystanders often stepped in to get her daughter off the fence and out of the tree. But Dye knew her daughter was doing important work: She was facing her fear and deciding whether to listen to it or push past it.

"Risky play teaches emotional resilience," says Jay Griffith, author of *A Country Called Childhood.* "To prevent small risk-taking in our children is to keep them infantile, enclosed, and unimaginative."[2]

Now, Griffith is not suggesting that we let them fence with real swords, or jump from a dangerous height in the hopes they'll sprout wings. But he is saying that in their pretend play, in their scaling of play structures in ways parents don't like, in their roaming the neighborhood in packs, they are doing important, essential, life-giving work. They are testing their sense of freedom and deciding what exactly they can handle. They are learning to deal with adversity, and developing their grit, their resolve, their pluck. Critical traits for children, but no less important for adults.

Unfortunately children today are growing up in a very different era than the one that sent them outdoors at the age of five and told them to be home by dark. A recent study of parents in the United Kingdom found that 43 percent of parents didn't think children under the age of fourteen should be allowed outside unsupervised.[3]

Seriously?

Yes, taking risks sometimes leads to danger. But the return is surprise, delight, growth. Risk leads to confidence, triumph, and an overwhelming sense that we can do what we set our minds to. In fact, some psychologists believe that the rise in anxiety and behavioral problems in children today stems from this lack of free play and risk-taking in early childhood.

As adults, we rarely get back to the kind of freedom we experienced in childhood. Biologically, we become more risk averse as we age. As we mature, our prefrontal cortex, the part of our brain that prevents us from acting on impulse and inhibits risk-taking, begins to put on the brakes and make us think twice before speaking up or stepping in. While that serves us in some ways, it also holds us back, reins us in, puts us in shackles, and encourages us to play small.

We fall for the lie of thinking it's better to endure the ache of mediocrity than to strive for greatness and risk the sting of genuine disappointment.

But we hunger for lives that are free. We long to be back in the game.

So let's get back to living in a way where we are playing to win. Where we go after victory with everything we've got.

True Victory

When I had four kids under the age of eight, sometimes my primary job as a husband was to give my wife a couple of hours reprieve from the constant demands of parenting.

So one summer day I decided to take my kids to a nearby park. As we began to take over the playground, we heard shouting in the distance. Wanting to see what the commotion was all about, we wandered over to discover a soccer field.

From behind the fence, we saw the source of the shouting. Like a drill sergeant, the soccer coach yelled commands and angrily blew his whistle when his players weren't following his instructions perfectly. We laughed at his intensity. I warned my kids that if they didn't start listening to me, I was going to get a whistle to use at home.

And then the coach's whistle screamed out one more time, followed by this command: "Stop what you are doing. Stop it! Come on, damn it!"

The players halted where they were, hung their heads, and circled up around the coach. Once he had their undivided attention, he yelled, "If you wanna win in the game, you gotta practice like it matters! Do you hear me? Like it matters, damn it!"

Now, there is no doubt that the manner in which we practice influences how we show up to play the game. And when you offer your time as a coach, you should rightly demand the respect of your players. There is a time to challenge players to give a little more, to try a little harder, to do a little better. There is even a time for anger.

But it was July, the middle of summer; it was late in the afternoon on a hot and humid day, and near the end of practice. And the players were seven- and eight-year-old kids.

As we turned away from the practice and headed back to the playground, I shook my head. That was one way to coach, one way to lead, one way to prepare for the upcoming game.

But while the best coaches in soccer, and in life, may insist on practicing like it matters and strive to win games, they also know that real victory is about so much more than a scoreboard.

Soccer was one of the first physical activities I returned to after relearning to walk. My legs were wrapped with Ace bandages because the skin on them was so fragile. To further protect them, I wore two pairs of bright-red sweatpants under my gold soccer shorts.

I know. It wasn't a great look.

I could barely run. My arms were still frozen at 90-degree angles. This little dude was a threat to no one on that field but himself and his own team!

Even so, Coach Steiner treated me like every other player. I was welcomed back, encouraged to practice to the best of my ability, and even invited to participate in our first game.

Near the end of that game, we were tied when our team had an opportunity for a penalty kick. Everyone gathered around in excitement, eager to see who Coach Steiner would choose. We expected him to select his best shooter, line the kid up, score the goal, and win.

That's what it's all about, after all.

And then I heard him call my name.

"Johnny, come over here."

I stood up and shuffled over to him, apprehensive about why he had called me over. Even with all the beautiful naïveté of childhood still coursing through my veins, I recognized that I had no business taking this kick. Every single other player on my team had a higher likelihood of scoring a goal than me.

Coach must have sensed how I felt because his first words to me were, "John, look at me."

I looked up.

He put his hand on my shoulder, bent down to eye level, held my gaze, and said, "You are the one I need for this, John. I need you to run out there, hold your head high, and kick that ball as hard as you can."

With that, he stood up, patted me on the back, and proclaimed, "Now John, go get us a victory."

I jogged off in my sweatpants and gold shorts. Stood behind the penalty line. I stared at the keeper. I would have sworn he was three hundred yards away.

The referee set down the ball and backpedaled toward the sideline.

I heard the sound of the whistle.

I took a deep breath, stumbled toward the ball, and took a mighty shot, using every ounce of strength that remained in my legs to launch that ball as hard as I could. I prayed it would make it to the goalie. I knew I wouldn't make the goal, but I at least wanted to make it far enough for the goalie to block it.

The ball slowly trundled toward the left goal post. The goalie took a couple of quick steps to his right, and dove to grab it, his hands outstretched. But somehow, some way, the ball snuck just past him and into the back of the net.

Goal!

I stared in shock. My teammates rushed over to congratulate me.

I had done it. I had scored the winning shot.

Looking back on that penalty kick, on that goal, and on the mob of kids that surrounded me afterward, I'll never forget that moment. Because we won.

No, I don't mean we won the game. I don't actually remember what the final score was.

The victory didn't happen when I scored the goal.

We won that day because our coach had the audacity to line up a skinny, burned, bent-over ten-year-old kid to show every player, every coach, and every parent on the bleachers what real victory looks like.

Sometimes victory comes from overcoming an enemy, defeating an opponent, or trouncing the other team. But other times victory means more than a win: it comes when you beat the odds, succeed in overcoming a struggle, or come together for a cause greater than yourself.

Coach Steiner wasn't going to let me sit on the sidelines anymore. He wasn't worried about whether I could kick that ball all the way to the goal, let alone past the goalie. He was concerned about showing me that I was still in the game, still on the team, and I still mattered. He taught me that in participating fully we all win; that in risking, we discover what we are truly capable of.

Victory comes when we take responsibility for our lives and stop waiting for others to do the work we are called to do.

Therein lies true freedom.

There is a reason that our justice system punishes people by taking away their freedom.

Freedom is a human need, like food and water.

For too long, we've forgotten how life-giving it is.

So here's a question to consider: Are you living free?

Okay, so you may not be locked in a cell. But do you feel free? Unfettered? Able to step forward, willing to risk it all?

We may think we're free, but I think we've gotten used to living shackled.

We've grown accustomed to being bound by debt, unfulfilling work, or low expectations.

We are chained to past hurts, tied down by limiting beliefs, or suffocated by the inability to forgive, accept, move forward.

And we accept an existence of playing small, stop dreaming, and merely tolerate a life that isn't fully ours.

So instead of sprinting into each day with the freedom to choose how we think, speak, act, and love, we let other people, unimportant things, or our own fear, run the show.

The greatest triumph in life is not competing and winning, but stepping into the arena and giving it your all.

It isn't easy or pain free. You may fall and fail. But it will make you feel alive.

And it will liberate you to live In Awe.

28

Showing Up

UNLESS SOMEONE LIKE YOU
CARES A WHOLE AWFUL LOT,
NOTHING IS GOING TO GET BETTER.
IT'S NOT.

Dr. Seuss, *The Lorax*

We were driving to baseball practice.

Henry, just six at the time, was a bit apprehensive. Outside of the occasional backyard wiffle ball game, he'd never played organized baseball and he didn't really know any of the kids on the team. He looked out the window, the weight of the world on his shoulders, as we neared the ball field.

"Little man," I began, "are you doing okay?"

He sighed deeply and responded, "I guess I'm just nervous."

He turned his gaze to the rearview mirror of the car. We locked eyes and he added, "Dad, the hardest part is just going. Once I'm there, I'll be fine. But Dad, going is scary."

My little man had it right.

Going is scary.

Showing up is the hard part.

But once we're there, we're glad we faced our fear, pushed it aside, and stepped up to the plate.

Henry was aware of this important truth at the age of six. I was twenty-four years old when I finally learned this lesson.

I've always been a slow learner.

It was early in the morning and I was getting ready for work. When the phone rang and I saw my mom's number, I knew that something must have happened because she never called that early.

She asked if I'd heard the news. Jack Buck had died. She wanted to make sure I knew, and to let me know that a Buck family member had called the house to invite me to his funeral.

I felt like I'd been punched in the gut.

Now, sporting fans around the country knew of Jack Buck. He was a spectacular sportscaster, so highly regarded that he'd been inducted into various Halls of Fame, including those for Major League Baseball, the National Football League, and the National Radio Hall of Fame.

And while he may have been known nationally, he was beloved in St. Louis. Jack was the voice of baseball for generations of St. Louis Cardinals fans. For nearly fifty years, his deep, raspy voice brought the play-by-play action of baseball to millions of fans.

Jack was royalty, but he was far from some distant celebrity to me.

Jack Buck was one of the reasons I was alive.

Let me tell you a little about this remarkable man.

This was a man who learned about a tragic fire that had engulfed a nine-year-old boy the very night it happened. Even though he had never met me, the following day he came to visit. Jack walked into my hospital room and saw a little boy tied down to a bed, burns on his entire body, unable to see, tethered to machines, and wrapped from head to toe in bandages.

This was a man who lost his breath at that first sight, before composing himself and pulling a chair across the tile floor so he could sit down right next to my bed. My eyes were swollen shut, so I didn't know who had just entered my room until I heard a cough and then a very familiar voice: "Kid. Wake up. You are going to live. You are going to survive. Keep fighting. When you get out of here we're going to celebrate you at the stadium. We'll call it John O'Leary Day at the ballpark, and it will make all this worthwhile." There was a long pause before he added, "Kid, are you listening to me? Keep fighting."

This was a man who somberly left my room after that first visit, made his way down the hall before pausing and leaning his head against a wall, letting the emotion catch up with him. The staff consoled him, but said there was no chance that I'd survive.

Undeterred, Jack came back and visited the following day, in spite of my dire prognosis. "Kid. Wake up. You are going to live. You are going to survive. Keep fighting. John O'Leary Day at the ballpark will make it all worthwhile. Keep fighting." His voice became a constant over the five months I spent in the hospital. He visited too many times to count.

This was a man who kept the promise of John O'Leary Day at the ballpark. He met our family at the stadium, proudly pushed me around in my wheelchair, introduced me to every player, and allowed me to broadcast part of the game with him. While I was seated next to him in the booth, he saw the scars, the bandages, the wheelchair, and the many struggles that remained for me. He also saw the joy, the grit, and the possibility that endured.

This was a man who, rather than accept that I'd never be able to hold anything with my damaged hands, sent a baseball to my home the next day, signed by a Cardinals player, with a note: "Kid, if you want a second baseball, you'll have to write a thank-you letter to the guy who signed the first one." With the help of my parents, I held a pen between my bandaged hands, sent a thank-you letter to the player, and, in doing so, took a mighty step toward returning to normalcy.

This was the man who followed through on that promise and sent me a second signed baseball.

After a second thank-you note, he sent a third baseball.

Then a fourth. (Are you seeing where this is going?)

Ultimately Jack Buck, an incredibly busy guy, made the time to send sixty baseballs to a little boy with no fingers.

In doing so, Jack Buck taught me how to write again.

Which means he was one of the reasons I was able to return to school.

This was a man who received the highest honor in Major League Baseball when he was inducted into the Baseball Hall of Fame the summer after I was burned. He received a crystal baseball to commemorate the honor. Twelve years later, he came to my college graduation to drop off a gift. It was his priceless crystal Hall of Fame baseball. I was twenty-two, directionless, unemployed, and probably still groggy from being out late the night before. I had no idea who I really was or what I might do in life. And he gave it to me.

This was a man who struggled mightily with Parkinson's disease for years and then was diagnosed with stage four cancer. This incredible man, who was so full of life, slowly withered in a hospital bed for the final five months of his life.

During the end of his life, as he suffered for five months in a hospital bed—the same amount of time as I'd spent in one as a child—how many times did I visit him?

The truth I'm about to share still pains me to admit seventeen years later. I hate to put these words to paper.

Not once.

I didn't visit Jack one single time.

It wasn't because of my demanding schedule. It wasn't that I was indifferent to all he'd done for me. It wasn't that I was ignorant of the mighty struggles he was facing. It wasn't because I was too arrogant or preoccupied. I certainly thought of and prayed for him daily during that time.

So why not write him?

Why not call?

Why not just show up at the hospital, walk to his room, step through the door, pull up a chair, sit beside him, and say, *Kid, wake up. You saved my life. You are why I write. You are why I went back to school. You are why I am where I am today. You changed the arc of my life. Kid, are you listening to me? Keep fighting.*

Why didn't I do that?

I wasn't free. No, I don't mean with my time, but with my mindset, my sense of self, my belief in my own value. I never went to visit my friend because I had an excuse we all use when we live in fear: *Someone else will do it.*

Somebody else will go. People with bigger titles. People who are better friends. People who are more important, more connected, more impactful than me will go visit.

And when that excuse wore out, the voice of fear whispered another lie: *Some other time. Tomorrow I'll visit. Next week.*

I kept putting it off.

And then I missed my chance.

That's why my heart broke when I got the call from my mom.

You'd think that after my mom's call, after learning that Jack had died, I would have learned the lesson, right?

I think you know the answer.

Four days later, as I pulled into the parking lot for the funeral, preparing to pay my last respects to my friend, it happened again.

I took a deep breath.

Straightened my tie.

Turned off the car.

And noticed a black Mercedes parked next to me. Stepping out of it was a Hall of Fame football player. A man who broadcast NFL games on television nationally and was a close friend of Jack's.

I glanced behind me.

Walking past were the owners of the St. Louis Cardinals. They ran a billion-dollar business, had influence, fame, and wealth. As they made their way into the church, they waved at another group of friends approaching.

From the front seat of my Jeep, I began taking inventory of what I saw around me.

Expensive cars.

Celebrities.

Current baseball players.

Former All-Stars.

Family members.

In other words, these were Jack's friends. People of worth, value, substance. The type of people who had showed up at the hospital. The type of friends who were with him when it actually counted.

I slumped back in my seat, defeated.

Think back to a moment in your life when you realized you didn't belong. Maybe while you were competing in a sporting event where everyone else was faster, better, or twice your size? Or on your first day at a new school when everyone else seemed to know the answer, and you didn't even understand the question? Or when you walked into a new job and felt the steep learning curve ahead of you and feared that you'd never catch up?

Well, that day I looked at those important people and realized that they had been with Jack during the good days and had shown up during the bad days.

I stared at my reflection in the rearview mirror. I saw the kid he'd visited dozens of times in the hospital. I saw a young man who didn't visit once when the roles were reversed. I saw a fake, an outsider, someone who just didn't measure up.

I turned the car back on, reversed out of my parking spot, and drove away. Yeah, you read that correctly.

Not only did I not visit Jack in the hospital; I didn't even go to his funeral. But this time, as I drove away, I knew what I was doing was wrong. And I began to cry.

You might think that twenty-four-year-old men are incredibly in touch with their feelings. That at that age we are willing to share the deep secrets we keep, and the truth of our emotions.

Yeah, right.

Before that day, like most guys my age, I had perfected the art of keeping everything bottled up, pushed down, under control.

I didn't tell people how I felt, what I needed, or how they impacted me.

But on that drive, I stopped trying to keep it all inside. I pulled over to the side of the road as the tears coursed down my cheeks.

I thought back to all the times he'd visited, all the gifts he'd given me, all the lessons he'd taught. How had I missed my chance to repay a small part of it? I had chosen to not show up, to never really thank him, to never say goodbye. To never tell a man who loved me well that I loved him back.

On the side of the road, with sobs racking my body, I felt the utter enormity of my mistake.

And I made a commitment to never let that happen again.

No more regrets.

No more fear.

No more hiding who I was and how I felt.

No more sideline living.

I looked at my watch. It was too late to make it to the funeral. But I would do something else. Take other steps. I would never again pass up an opportunity to tell someone I love them, skip a chance to visit someone in need, overlook an occasion to utter the words "I'm sorry" or "thank you" or "I love you."

I made the commitment to live more bravely, fearlessly, and freely.

To my everlasting regret, I wasn't able to live like this while Jack Buck was alive.

But he had helped me once more, this time from the grave.

Waking Up

On the morning of Jack Buck's funeral, as I drove away from the church, I drove toward my grandparents' house, where my family gathered to enjoy Sunday dinners, birthday parties, and holiday celebrations. Grandma and Grandpa were the classic couple from the Greatest Generation, humble, faithful, hardworking, and patriotic. As they neared their sixtieth anniversary they were still wild about each other.

For the first time in my life I stopped by unannounced. When they answered the door you'd have thought Publishers Clearing House was there to let them know they'd just won $10 million. Emphatically, they wondered what I was doing there before joyfully inviting me in. We visited for a couple of hours and had lunch together. Before leaving I thanked them not only for lunch but for being two people I respect dearly, love greatly, and long to be more like. I hugged them, thanked them again, and told them I loved them. They knew it already, but I wanted them to hear it clearly from me.

Freedom.

The next evening I took my parents to dinner. It's easy to lose touch with those you love the most in the busyness of life. I wanted to take time to thank them for all they did for me. They had been my constant advocates during my darkest days and my cheerleaders during the brightest ones. I wanted them to know the extent to which I respected and loved them. They were my heroes when I was a little kid growing up, but I wanted them to know that they still were. Those were hard words for a twenty-four-year-old to say out loud, but seeing their faces afterward made it worthwhile.

Freedom.

Later that month, Jack Buck's widow graciously met with me so I could share the profound impact her husband had made on my life. While Jack, years earlier, had told Carol about what I'd been through—the fire and the recovery—he'd never told her about the repeated visits to the hospital, or John O'Leary Day at the ballpark, or the sixty signed baseballs, or the crystal Hall of Fame baseball. She was blown away. She shared that hearing the story made her husband come back to life for a moment. She hugged and thanked me.

More freedom.

I then wrote Jack a long letter of apology for not being the friend to him that he'd been to me. I recounted all the things he'd done for me as a child, all the times he'd visited, all the love he'd given me, and how his actions had changed my life. With that letter in hand, I took his son, Joe Buck, out to coffee. At a packed coffee shop in St. Louis, seated across from Joe, with tears clouding my eyes, I read the long letter I wrote to his dad. It was difficult to get through. But it was also incredibly liberating.

More freedom.

As a burn patient I had vowed that when I got out of the hospital I was never going to go back. That intense fear of hospitals and the painful memories of what I had endured in them lingered. It was one more layer that had kept me from showing up to visit Jack. But I was no longer going to let that fear keep me from entering into important moments in the lives of people I loved. Sometimes the very best way to overcome a fear is to dive directly into it. So I trained for twelve months to become a hospital chaplain and spent three amazing years visiting with kids like me, who were facing extreme difficulty but who were also learning firsthand the power of genuine courage, resiliency, and hope.

You guessed it: more freedom.

Embracing the power of mentorship—something I'd learned from Jack—I became active with an organization that does exactly that. Big Brothers Big Sisters matches children who might benefit from a positive adult role model with adults willing to make a difference. Jack's mentorship is why I became a Big Brother. It's why I served as an ambassador for the organization. It's why I am active today on the board of advisors for BBBS.

Only after Jack's death did I slowly begin sharing my story. I'd been asked to relate it before, but had never felt sufficiently worthy, capable, or ready. It took me fifteen years to tell the story of what happened on that January day when I caught fire. First I shared it with a group of three Girl Scouts. (I know. I was pretty big-time.) Then, with a group of twelve volunteers. Followed by a meeting with twenty retirees. It started extraordinarily small, but the important part is that it started. As groups continued to invite me to speak, I began to realize how life-giving it was to own my scars and share my story. I took a leap of faith and turned a side gig into a lifelong mission. What has kept me incredibly humble and hungry as that mission has grown is recognizing where this story began: with the reality that one person can in fact change the world, and has the daily opportunity to do more with whatever they've been given. It's a message that has everything to do with what we can accomplish together when we are brave enough to just show up.

And finally, it's why, when Beth and I were blessed with our first child, we sought to name him after someone we hoped he'd emulate.

We named him Jack.

Jack Buck influenced me profoundly during his life. But, ironically, he may have saved his greatest lesson for me for after his death.

You see, when I was in the hospital he'd begun every visit with the words "Kid, wake up." It took Jack's death for me to finally heed those words.

I stopped living chained to the bench. I finally stepped forward and owned that my life was a gift and could still be used for good.

It turns out that when you reawaken your sense of freedom, you stop giving in to fear, stop existing on the sidelines; you stop saying "somebody else" and "some other time." You start risking bigger, daring greatly, accepting accountability. You start recognizing that *this* is the time, that *you* are the one, and that the best is yet to come.

And it is then that you'll recognize the truth of what Henry told me on the way to his first baseball practice: Once you show up, once you're finally there, you realize that you are fine.

Going may be a bit scary.

But it's worth it.

29

Sing Out Loud

NO ACT OF KINDNESS, NO MATTER HOW SMALL, IS EVER
WASTED.

Aesop, "The Lion and the Mouse"

"Have you ever been made fun of?" a young woman asked me.
We were at a school outside of Minneapolis. The tone of the
student's voice and the look on her face hinted that she knew how it
felt to bear the brunt of someone else's joke.

With fifteen hundred high school students staring at me, I answered her question by asking one of the entire student body: "What
do you all think? Have any of you ever been made fun of?"

No hands went up.

I had forgotten: These were teenagers. They needed a bit of playful encouragement to engage.

"Come on," I chided, "if you've ever been picked on, made fun
of, put down, or bullied, raise your hand."

Nearly every hand went up.

"How many of you have seen others being made fun of?"

Nearly every hand went up again.

I nodded. An astonishing 70.6 percent of students report witnessing bullying.

Before finally answering her question, I asked one more of the students: "How many of you have spoken up when someone was being made fun of?"

A small smattering of hands appeared. But the vast majority of the students shifted uncomfortably in their seats.

This wasn't surprising. While everyone has witnessed unkindness, we also know that speaking up means taking a risk. It means potentially relinquishing popularity to do what is right.

But speaking up makes a huge difference. When a bystander intervenes, 57 percent of the time the bullying stops within seconds.[1]

With just a few words, you can change someone's life.

This is true in our schools.

It's also true in our communities, offices, and homes.

Think about it. How often have you witnessed someone being treated rudely, put down, or belittled at work? What about at a store, a restaurant, or elsewhere in your community? How about online?

Now that all of our hands are up, how often have you stepped forward, spoken up, or intervened?

My friend, our human tendency is to seek to fit in and be a part of the crowd rather than step in and stand out. It stems from our ancestors' need to be a part of a tribe in order to survive. Thus, even today, our need to belong supersedes our desire to do what is right. The majority of us would rather be in the crowd going along with what we know is wrong than risk being ostracized for speaking up for what we know is right.

So I shared with those students an experience from my junior year of high school. Sure, I hoped it answered that young woman's question, but more important, I hoped it would be a wake-up call about how essential it is to recognize we all have a voice.

We can remain silent, or we can use it to speak up. And in doing so, change the world. Yes, it's that important.

When I was sixteen, weighing in at a whopping ninety-six pounds, dealing with acne, teeth bristling with braces, with a body covered with scars, I was an easy target. So it isn't surprising that one of the biggest kids at my school—a football player who was athletic, good-looking, funny, and popular—decided to start making fun of me.

The first time it happened, when he made a comment about my hands, I just ignored it. I pretended it wasn't that big a deal. I put my head down. Walked past him. End of story. High school stuff.

And then it happened the following day.

And the one after that.

Every time he'd pass me in the hallways, the lunchroom, or a classroom he'd mock my hands and ridicule my scars. He'd make fun of the way I walked, the way I looked, and what I'd been through.

You learn a lot of lessons growing up with five siblings. How to share. How to argue. How to find the one thing that annoys your siblings the most.

Another lesson you learn is that if you ever let on that something they say bothers you, they'll say it again. And again.

So I ignored him and kept quiet and hoped it would stop.

But it didn't.

Each afternoon I'd leave school, go home, and act normal, but feel absolutely crushed. It wasn't because I was getting picked on. It was the knowledge that he was right.

I was burned.

My hands were different.

My skin was ugly.

I wasn't like every other kid in school.

I had never dated, and probably never would.

I was unlovable.

Listen, after years of reflection and prayer, with the unconditional love of my wife, support of my family, blessed perception of my kids, and innumerable experiences of being accepted, I've learned to celebrate who I am.

But back then, when I was an easily influenced adolescent trying to fit in, this bully's nasty perspective of me became my reality.

I believed his words.

As adolescents, our sense of self often stems from the way our peers feel about us.

But don't kid yourself. Too often that remains the case even as we age.

The cruelty continued for weeks. My friends knew, classmates overheard, teachers were aware. But no one spoke up.

And then it happened.

Seventh period. World history class. Once again, the voice began pestering me from behind.

The teacher was at the chalkboard; I just lowered my head to take it, not expecting anything to be done.

But then the smallest kid in class, Jason, got up from his desk and walked past me over to the bully. He pointed at the big, tough, athletic, popular kid and yelled in a high-pitched, squeaky voice: "Dude!"

The entire class stopped what they were doing and stared.

The squeaky voice continued, "Shut up! You have no idea what this kid has been through." With his index finger outstretched at the big, tough bully, Jason repeated, "Shut up!"

The class was stunned.

We all waited to see what would happen next in this modern-day reenactment of David and Goliath. Except this time, David didn't have a slingshot. He didn't have five smooth stones. And he didn't have an army standing at the ready behind him.

Those who were in the class with me that day will never forget what happened: The big guy put his hands together, bowed his head, and didn't even mutter a word. Never again did he ridicule me or anyone else in the school.

That day, Jason, a classmate I rarely even spoke to, heard the calling to be courageous. He used his voice when I didn't feel able to utilize mine, and changed my life.

Despite the social pressure, despite the fear undoubtedly whispering in his ear to stay seated, Jason stood up, shook off the shackles, and realized that he had the power to make the right choice.

That, to me, is freedom.

The ability to know something isn't right.

To recognize no one else is doing anything about it.

And to step in and do it yourself, utilizing your voice, your presence, your very life for a cause greater than yourself.

I didn't have freedom back then, but I'm striving to embrace it more today. Because I don't want you to be like me, stuck in your seat. I want you to embrace your power to choose to speak up for yourself, and for those who don't yet have the freedom to do so.

Oliver Wendell Holmes tells us, "When a resolute young fellow steps up to the great bully, the World, and takes him boldly by the beard, he is often surprised to find it come off in his hand, and that it was only tied on to scare away the timid adventurers."[2]

What Jason did on my behalf inspires me to this day. He taught me that we all have a choice. To be timid adventurers and let obstacles and other people hold us back, shut us down, and keep us small. Or to reawaken our sense of freedom that helps us remember that we were born to be brave, we were born to be bold, and the world needs us to raise our voices, enter the conversation, and change the world.

One squeaky voice at a time.

What begins as a faint, courageous whisper can turn into a mighty, transformative roar. We're witnessing the power of raising our voices through many social movements today. As abuse survivors refuse to stay quiet, behavior that once was tolerated is no longer accepted. As single voices join together, they call out for gender equality, diversity, and inclusion. Voices are positively affecting national laws, corporate policies, and conversations around the community.

Where do you need to raise your voice? At work? At home? In your community? Is there something you see that isn't right or needs to be addressed? Who is begging for your defense, your encouragement, or your love?

Freedom doesn't mean living selfishly, foolishly, or recklessly.

It doesn't mean you live without concerns, throw caution to the wind, and live without fear. That's not freedom. That's carelessness.

As Jason showed us, freedom means actually knowing what matters, taking responsibility for your life, and then exercising your power of choice. Yes, you'll realize the consequences of standing up and the risk of living boldly. But rather than living not to lose, you choose to give it your all.

Just Say No

The collection plate was making its rounds.

Years ago Beth and I decided to give to the church electronically. It ensures we can be intentional on the front end and consistently give throughout the year. Even so, at church we want to be an example for our kids, so we usually drop a few dollars in the offering plate.

I had just returned from giving a speech that included book sales, so my wallet was a bit fatter than usual. As the collection plate reached our pew, I passed some money to the kids so they could each put something in. Patrick, seated next to me, saw the contents of my wallet, looked at me, and then asked in a voice that echoed throughout the church, "How much are you going to give, Dad?"

I whispered back, "How much do you think we should give?"

With his brown eyes sparkling, he loudly responded, "Give it all!"

Now, my first reaction was, *Patrick. Not happening. Are you crazy? We give electronically anyway. We give enough. Here, be a good little boy, and put these three dollars in.*

But then I looked at my boy, saw his generous spirit, then back at the plate in front of me. I exhaled deeply and emptied the contents of my wallet into the plate, feeling far lighter than I had before entering church. And somehow far richer, too.

Give it all. It is a concept that kids are familiar with. They leave it all on the table. They give every game their whole heart. They don't hold back or conserve energy. They are fully spent at the end of the day, with nothing left in the tank.

My friend, why do we stop giving it all? Risking where we are today for what our lives could be tomorrow? Why do we stop emptying ourselves fully each and every day?

Why don't we reach for the job promotion?

Pursue that quick weekend away?

Get to the office a little early to help a team member get ahead on that project, or visit an old friend, or say hello to the new neighbors?

Why don't we take that class we've always wanted to try?

Do something radically new?

Lay our heads down at night fully spent, with no regrets?

We've lost sight of the freedom that is our birthright. We've forgotten the joy of taking charge of our days, respectfully speaking our minds, and claiming whatever path feels like the one that will lead not to goals scored or games won, but to a life of genuine fulfillment.

Let me tell you about someone who knew what it meant to live this way.

William Borden was destined for a life of privilege. His father ran the Borden conglomerate and had accumulated massive wealth. Little William was the heir to this empire and was groomed from a young age to assume the leadership of these businesses.

He excelled in high school. He was athletic, popular, and an outstanding student. While I finished high school in the half of the class that made the top half possible, young Borden finished at the very top of his.

After he had graduated and gained admission into Yale, family friends presented him with a small Bible. He brought it with him on a trip around the world before he began his studies at Yale.

While traveling, Borden realized how much wealth his family truly possessed. He saw firsthand the struggle most people in the world went through simply to put food on the table. Rather than follow the golden path set out for him, he committed to being part of the solution.

In his Bible, Borden wrote a simple phrase, just two words, to guide him on the next step of his life: "No reserves."

To Borden this was a reminder to make sure he was using everything he had, every gift, every insight, every ounce of compassion. To not reserve anything, but to put it all out there, and be a light in the world.

Heeding the simple motto he wrote down, while at Yale, Borden helped found an organization called Yale Hope Mission, with a focus on serving the disadvantaged in the community. As a freshman, he organized a Bible study and invited classmates to join him. By the end of his freshman year, 125 classmates had participated. By the time he graduated from Yale, more than a thousand students attended such groups, a stunning number, considering Yale had a total enrollment of 1,350.

Upon graduating, Borden wrote a second note in the front of his Bible: "No retreat."

Though everyone expected him to return home and begin learning the family business, this phrase became his mantra as he walked away from it, toward a life in service to the poor of the world. When his family encouraged him to come home, these words reminded him to stand fast, push forward, and make his vision a reality. He was all in.

Borden moved to Egypt. Shortly after arriving there, he contracted spinal meningitis. Three weeks later he was dead.

He was twenty-five.

The son of privilege was buried in a simple grave in Egypt. So little did he possess, that it all fit in a simple wooden trunk. His belongings were ferried across the ocean to his distraught family. One of the items was the Bible he had received upon graduating from high school. As his mother opened the first page, she found the notes he had scribbled in the front to remind himself of his purpose: "No reserves. No retreat."

But there was a final note she noticed, two additional words written just a few days before his death.

A world away from the one where he grew up, knowing the end was near, Borden wrote: "No regrets."

He didn't look back on his life with remorse; he didn't view his life as a disappointment. He knew what mattered most. He was steadfast in what was worthy of living for, clear on what he was fighting for, and certain of what he'd be willing to die for.

This isn't shared in hopes that you'll live counter to all your peers, sell all your belongings, and move halfway across the world from your family. No, I share it to encourage you to imagine the freedom of going through each day with these words tattooed on your heart: *No reserves. No retreat. No regrets.*

Don't get to the end of your journey and realize the life you lived was not yours. Don't forget that you are free to choose. Right now.

You aren't thrilled with the way things are moving forward in your relationships, in your career, or in your health? You don't like the direction things are taking in your family, community, or country? You have the freedom to sit back, stay silent, and curse the problem. Or stand up, speak out, and strive to make it better.

There is always a better way.

It may require forging a new path.

It isn't always popular.

But it will allow you to live with no reserves, no retreat, and no regrets.

The choice is yours.

30

Get in the Game

AND SO FOR A TIME, IT LOOKED AS IF ALL THE ADVENTURES
WERE COMING TO AN END; BUT THAT WAS NOT TO BE.

C. S. Lewis, *The Lion, the Witch and the Wardrobe*

The entire hallway was lined with pictures of Hall of Fame base-ball players, some of the greatest hitters, pitchers, and fielders who ever played the game. But my attention was focused on one picture in particular: a photo of Jack Buck.

Lost in reflection, I was startled when I heard, "Are you ready?" It was the general manager of the St. Louis Cardinals, Mike Girsch.

Looking away from the picture and at Mike, I smiled and said, "Yeah, I'm ready. Let's do this."

We walked down a hallway, made a turn, and entered the St. Louis Cardinals' clubhouse. And it was as if I was transported to a day thirty years earlier, when I'd first entered that doorway: August 26, 1987.

After I'd spent five months in the hospital, and some additional months at home recovering, Jack Buck had kept the promise of John O'Leary Day at the ballpark. We watched batting practice from the field and visited with the coaches in the dugout. As my dad pushed the wheelchair, Jack guided him and a wide-eyed, awestruck little boy through the door that read PLAYERS ONLY CLUBHOUSE.

As the players prepared for the game, in various stages of undress, a stunned but joy-filled little boy got to meet his heroes, get their autographs, and be welcomed into their family. It was a day I will never forget.

Three decades later, the anxiety and butterflies that I'd felt as a kid remained, but this time, rather than being rolled in, I walked upright into the clubhouse.

The players were seated in front of a whiteboard. The president of the Cardinals, John Mozeliak, spoke to his team about the challenges of the upcoming season, the certainty of adversity, and the need to be mentally tough enough to embrace it, to rise above it, and to be better because of it.

He told them that no one embodied this more than the speaker he had invited today. He then asked his team to welcome his friend John O'Leary.

As I walked to the front of the room and prepared to speak, I couldn't shake the memory of me as a little boy. The St. Louis Cardinals were not just heroes to me as a boy, but symbolized so much more. Before the fire, I'd been convinced that one day I'd join their ranks. Even after that dream died, my family continued gathering around the radio, listening to the games, cheering the exploits of our team. We often visited the ballpark to root for the team in person. That passion for baseball was now passed down to my children.

And here I was, standing before a new generation of players, most not even born the last time I was in this room.

These successful, supremely talented athletes leaned forward in their chairs. As they listened to all I'd been through, and heard about the people who'd stepped in to make a miracle happen, including a legend in their franchise, they laughed, cried, and asked questions. They then committed to doing even more, both on and off the field.

At the end of the meeting, the players formed a line, all holding copies of my first book, *On Fire*. As each one approached, we shook hands, hugged, and I got to do something I could never have imagined as a child: I gave my autograph to each of the St. Louis Cardinals!

Seriously. In what world does that happen?

It was a surreal moment, a memory I will cherish forever.

As I said my goodbyes and thanked them for the opportunity to speak to them, they asked if I'd be willing to come back later that summer and join them on the field on the thirtieth anniversary of John O'Leary Day at the ballpark.

I responded that I appreciated the invite but was too busy. Perhaps somebody else might be interested. Maybe some other time.

Are you kidding? I said yes!

Full Circle

The thirtieth anniversary of that special day at the ballpark included an invitation onto the field before the game.

We took a family picture and met the players. One of them asked if I'd like to throw out the first pitch.

I gazed around the stadium, glanced toward the players stretching nearby, then looked at my hands. No wrist movement. No fingers. No ability to grasp the ball, to heave it forward. My elbows are still locked at about 90-degree angles. My shoulders have limited mobility.

In other words, there was no way for me to throw the first pitch successfully. It was simply impossible.

Until I looked at my kids.

Standing in her favorite spot, right next to me, was Grace. Her blond hair was pulled back, and her brilliant blue eyes sparkled through her glasses as she took in the commotion around her. This little girl taught me to rekindle that sense of immersion in life, to savor the moment, to play hard every day, to talk about my feelings, and to see my inherent worth. There was nothing to hide from, nothing to apologize for. After all, I'm her dad, and maybe I was burned when I was little, but I'm all better now. Perfect the way I am.

Next to her stood Henry. He is my spirited adventurer who wears his emotions on his sleeve. Trees are to be climbed, rocks are to be jumped off, life is to be explored passionately. He exudes a sense of belonging and still sees friends everywhere he looks. And because that's what he chooses to see, that's what he always finds. He sometimes gets scared, but he still shows up.

Next to Henry stood Patrick. He wore his Cardinals jersey and cap, his unofficial uniform of the summer. On his left hand, you guessed it, his faithful glove. The kid believes. He lives in the sense of expectancy, joyfully awaiting great things everywhere. Patrick knows the next event, game, day, trip is going to be awesome, and he's seldom disappointed. He shows up with that glove on his hand and a smile on his face and leaves a wake of joy in the lives of everyone he encounters.

My oldest, Jack, was at the end of the line. Here was my brave boy, my firstborn, the one who first taught me what it meant to be a father, what unconditional love actually feels like, and what it can inspire us to do. He was the first to rekindle within me a sense of wonder, and he extinguished my fears when he saw my stomach, covered with scars that were red, bumpy, and ridgy, but chose to love them anyway. Jack lives all-in and reminds me every time I see him of the magnificent man we named him after.

Just past Jack, I witnessed the unbounded beauty of my wife, Beth. With her brunette hair falling onto her shoulders, she turned and caught my gaze. A smile lit her face. She hadn't been at the stadium thirty years earlier, but she knew how much this meant to me, what it symbolized. Someone once told me that you'll never be more attracted to your spouse than on your wedding day. But every single time I see Beth I'm convinced she is more stunning, more striking, and more beautiful than the time before. She just keeps getting better, and I'm blown away that she chose *me,* and that she still does. She is the reason I have these children to love and to raise and to learn from.

Inspired by my family, I realized there was no way I could turn down this opportunity.

No reserves. No retreat. No regrets.

So I looked into the eyes of the ballplayer and told him firmly, "Yes. Let's do it!"

He handed me the ball.

As I awkwardly tried to balance the ball between my hands, I was immediately struck with the thought that I'd just made a terrible mistake. I could barely hold the ball, let alone pitch it.

With the August sun shining down, I wiped the sweat off my

forehead, staggered toward the mound, and began trying to think through how this was going to go down.

About halfway to the mound, there was a tug on my jersey. I turned around and saw Patrick staring up at me. His big brown eyes twinkled with life.

"Dad . . ."

There was a long pause.

"Don't embarrass us."

He then playfully patted me on the back.

Not what I need right now, Patrick!

I finished my march toward the mound. Waved to the crowd, in the hope of appearing calm, and waited for the catcher to get set.

I felt the ball between my hands, balanced it on the knuckles of my right hand, and said a prayer. Then I kicked my leg up and hurled the ball.

A packed Busch Stadium with more than forty-six thousand Cardinals fans saw a forty-year-old guy throw a perfect strike, to the surprise of the catcher. The only person more surprised than the crowd watching from their seats was the man who threw it! I practically danced off the mound, euphoric, shocked, grateful. Skipping over to home plate, I gave the catcher a hug.

And then walked back to my family, back to this motley crew that had taught me how to strive daily to embrace the freedom of living fully, of living In Awe. And I looked off to the side.

Like mighty pillars supporting the rest of us, I saw my first two teachers in life, my parents.

My mom. Her audacity in getting me to own my life that morning in the emergency room had saved me. Her insistence that I play the piano allowed me to look, beyond the horizon, for a future I could not yet see for myself. Through the ups and downs of my recovery, the inherent challenges of raising six kids, personal health issues, and difficulties in being the primary caretaker for my dad, she has unrelenting faith that has inspired me to believe in miracles, too. I walked over and gave her a big hug, then told her, "The reason I could throw that baseball was because you taught me that anything was possible. Thanks, Mom. I love you."

I then walked over to my dad.

Today he sat silently but resolutely in his wheelchair. He'd spent the past twenty-six years grappling with Parkinson's disease, the same disease Jack Buck had endured. My dad can no longer stand, or drive, or work. Speaking is incredibly difficult for him, and even swallowing food can present a challenge. Yet I know of no other person who has shown up as incessantly in my life, who has complained less, smiled more, in his refusal to surrender to adversity, than Dad.

Thirty years earlier, I was the one in a wheelchair and Dad pushed me around the stadium. Today I had the honor of pushing my dad.

Before we left the field to head back to the stands for an afternoon of watching the game, I bent down, hugged him, and said, "Dad, I love you. I want to be just like you when I grow up. Just like you."

We can learn a lot about how to love, lead, and live In Awe from children. But it's critically important to recognize that you don't need to be a child to rediscover and rekindle your childlike ability to unleash inspiration, meaning, and joy.

Each of us, every day, has a choice to reawaken these five childlike senses: To enter into each day with the wonder, curiosity, and questions of a child. To walk through life *expecting* awesome. To be fully immersed in the moment in front of us. To know that we belong and remain wildly, uncompromisingly open to new people, new ideas, and new experiences. And to skip forward freely, knowing that we were made not to sit back but to stand up, step in, and speak out in love.

The time is now.

The choice is yours.

The life you desire most, and the one you once enjoyed effortlessly as a child, can be yours again. The invitation to live In Awe awaits.

Sense #5: Freedom

Somebody else, some other time.
Or
No reserves, no retreat, no regrets.

I hope you are finished living someone else's life.
I hope you are ready to play to win.
I hope you realize the freedom that beckons if you can stop
listening to fear, and start racing forward, holding nothing back.
Think of how you felt when the school year was over
and three months of summer spread before you.
Recall the feeling of when you kicked off your shoes after a
long day and it was finally time to play.
Remember the joy that awakened
when you smiled broadly,
laughed frequently,
spoke honestly,
dreamed wildly,
and lived fully.
True victory is giving life your all.
We get one life.

While going is the hard part, it's also the best part.
So choose to stick up for others.
Share how you feel.
Take risks.
Fight giants and change the world.

It's time to unleash freedom, live bravely,
and get back into the game.
I'll see you on the field.

Awestruck

THE RAINBOW FISH SHARED HIS SCALES LEFT AND RIGHT. AND THE MORE HE GAVE AWAY, THE MORE DELIGHTED HE BECAME. WHEN THE WATER AROUND HIM FILLED WITH GLIMMERING SCALES, HE AT LAST FELT AT HOME AMONG THE OTHER FISH.

Marcus Pfister, *The Rainbow Fish*

Farmers have roosters. You may have an alarm clock. We have Henry.

Since he was three years old, Henry has always been the first one up in our house. He'd talk to himself in bed, build Lego structures in his room, or sing while playing with toys. Eventually he'd escape the confines of his room. Beth and I would hear the pitter-patter of his footsteps down the hallway, then notice them pause as he peered into our room before continuing down the hallway to his next adventure.

One morning he came sprinting from his room into ours. He ran over to me and pronounced loudly, "Dad, you gotta see this. Come on!"

Henry forced me out of bed, took my hand in his, and dragged me to our family room. He pulled back the curtains, and we stared out at the ash-gray early-morning sky. As he excitedly pointed out the window, I tried to pry my sleepy eyes open. At first I wasn't sure what he was pointing toward. But then, on the horizon, I saw it. And understood.

The light was beginning to push back the darkness. The night was transforming into day. And the sun was beginning its dance in the eastern sky.

He was giddy, astonished, in awe at the miracle of the morning sunrise.

That's one way to greet the start of a new day.

What about you? How do you respond to the rising of the sun? What's your mindset at the dawn of a new day?

For the overachievers already up, it's all too easy to ignore the sunrise entirely and stay focused on what tasks lie ahead. And the night owls punch the snooze button, angry at the alarm for waking them. They curse the light and try to go back to sleep.

Well, like Henry, I want to be enamored of, stunned by, and besotted with the majesty of each morning.

I want that passion not only for the sunrise, but for my work, my family, my faith, and my life.

My office decor helps remind me of this goal. You see, my office is covered in pictures. The entire wall behind my desk is filled with photos of family. There are pictures of my grandparents, parents, and siblings. There are photos of my wife, our kids, and our special moments together. These pictures remind me who I am, where I come from, and what truly matters.

On another wall are pictures of guests I've had on our *Live Inspired Podcast*. They are world-class writers and speakers, astronauts and business owners, thought leaders, overcomers and friends. These individuals have stories that inspire, and they lead lives that motivate me to better use my talents, share my resources, and impact others.

The wall opposite my desk includes photos of individuals who have profoundly shaped the world. There are pictures of Martin Luther King Jr., Abraham Lincoln, Mother Teresa, and others. They remind me that one person can in fact change the world if they dare to dream big and risk fully.

And to their left hangs my favorite picture of all. I believe it is the most important photograph taken in the history of the world.

It's called the Pale Blue Dot.

It was taken by NASA's Voyager I, which was originally launched in 1977 to photograph Saturn and Jupiter. The scientists imagined that Voyager I might last five years out in space. But it kept going. And going. Lasting more than forty years, it provided never-before-seen images of our entire solar system.

While every other picture in my office was taken a few feet away from the subject, the Pale Blue Dot was photographed from a bit farther back. In fact, the subject of this picture was captured from a distance of 4 billion miles.

The picture is grainy. It primarily shows the immensity of space. The vast darkness is pierced by innumerable small specks of light, revealing stars in the distance. Four beams of light from our sun cut through the center of the picture.

And hovering in one of those four rays, if you squint your eyes just right and look closely enough, you'll see a faint, barely perceptible pale blue dot.

That almost indiscernible orb is our planet. Even with the earth's mighty circumference of some 25,000 miles, even with more than 7 billion humans living on it, in this picture it's little more than a speck of dust. Carl Sagan, the great astronomer, succinctly sums up why this picture is so magnificently important:

> That's here. That's home. That's us. On it everyone you love, everyone you know, everyone you ever heard of, every human being who ever was, lived out their lives. The aggregate of our joy and suffering, thousands of confident religions, ideologies, and economic doctrines, every hunter and forager, every hero and coward, every creator and destroyer of civilization, every king and peasant, every young couple in love, every mother and father, hopeful child, inventor and explorer, every teacher of morals, every corrupt politician, every "superstar," every "supreme leader," every saint and sinner in the history of our species lived there—on a mote of dust suspended in a sunbeam.[1]

Well, it puts misplacing your keys in perspective, doesn't it?

In fact, when astronomers first journeyed into space and viewed our planet in its proper place for the very first time, they experienced what came to be called "the overview effect." It is a kind of mental clarity and awe that is experienced once we understand our place in the universe for the first time. While walking on the moon was a leap for humankind, it was the images of Earth that may have impacted us most. They show our place in the world, in the solar system, and in our vast universe.

They illustrate that we are one small part of something truly awe-inspiring.

That the world we inhabit is a small part of an eternal, unending, and expanding cosmic dance.

At first glance, you might think this suggests we are nothing more than minor players, unremarkable creatures, unimportant beings.

That's not how I see it, though. Not at all.

In fact, the awe of knowing our place in the world can do something powerful: It allows us to fully engage in the dance and give it our all.

Dacher Keltner, a professor of psychology at the University of California, Berkeley, has been studying awe for years. And his research shows that awe, a fundamental human emotion, is incredibly instructive.

Awe turns us away from self-absorption.

It attunes us to others.

It reminds us of our place in the world.

This in turn leads us to act differently, make better choices, and look for ways to benefit the world, instead of just ourselves.

The experience of awe makes us more likely to come to the aid of others.

Awe is a part of the human experience because it promotes a sense of the small self and turns us toward the greater good, the bigger picture. Awe goes back to our ancestral origins; it helps us live in groups successfully, peacefully, and collaboratively.

Today, spending less time in nature, we have less opportunity for awe. We rarely step outside to look up and around. While we sprint through each day living in the "busy," responding to the urgent, we frequently miss the gift of the moment, the majesty of embracing the truly important. We are therefore less attuned to the needs of others and more focused on our own little orb.

But cultivating these five senses, so alive in our children, will ensure awe once again and allow it to become a daily practice. Choosing to rekindle awe will not just impact your life, but create ripples that spread throughout the world.

When you reawaken your sense of wonder, you'll return to the path of possibility. Rather than clinging to your ego and the desire to have all the answers, you'll be bold enough to ask the kinds of questions that lead to thinking more creatively, collaborating more effectively, innovating more frequently, and proving the impossible possible. You may even find yourself hosting champagne and ice-cream parties with ferocious optimism.

When you recalibrate your sense of expectancy, you'll return to the potency of first-time living, viewing your days as a great adventure and everything within them as potentially awesome. You'll possess renewed hope for tomorrow and joyfully await its arrival. And in that hopeful anticipation, you'll actually attract the very things you imagine happening next. Just don't be surprised when you start bringing a baseball glove to the stadium.

When you get back in touch with your sense of immersion, you'll be engaged in the moment and recognize the beauty surrounding you. Rather than being overscheduled and overwhelmed, you'll slow down, look up at the clouds, get clear on what matters, and take action because of it. Renewed with more rest and frequent play, you'll be so effective professionally that you'll do better work and enjoy greater success. You'll also be so proud of your work, you'll want to put your name on it, take it home, and hang it on the fridge.

When you reconnect with your sense of belonging, you'll embrace the fact that although you may be different, may have endured struggles in the past, and may feel like an incredibly small piece that just doesn't fit, in reality you are an essential, valuable, priceless part of the puzzle. The contagion of joy will course through your veins with such veracity that you'll be able to quiet a bustling coffee shop, reminding people of a reason they should celebrate their lives: They belong.

And when you once again live with the sense of freedom that is your birthright, you'll be released from the chains that once bound you to previous mistakes, limiting beliefs, or the lie of timidity. You'll live with a mantra of no reserves, no retreat, and no regrets, holding nothing back, capable of accepting every opportunity, courageous enough to take worthwhile chances. You'll even be willing to step up to the giant, bravely use your voice, and make a difference that will change the world. Starting with your own.

My friend, the day is new and the sun is rising.

You choose where you go from here.

You can continue doing things the way you've been doing them. But instead, I hope you accept the invitation of awe.

It's time to unleash your inspiration, meaning, and joy.

And see what is possible when you live In Awe.

Hall of Heroes

Brian Buffini can "put his name on it" as a world-class speaker, coach, business owner—and an even better leader, husband, and dad.

There have been many emotional moments in my
speaking career. One of my absolute favorites
is the standing ovation my little friend Curtis received from
his future classmates. The fist bump was awesome, too.

All the chatting we did while driving through Ireland about
how lucky we were to simply be there eventually led to
further evidence of that truth: the Cliffs of Moher.

I feel pretty energetic and passionate about life. That
is, until I visit with Sister Buder!

Jack Buck gave me innumerable gifts for which I am forever
grateful, including a friendship with his son, Joe.

You never forget your first time—in particular, when it was playing the piano in front of an audience of twenty thousand at the MGM Grand!

Thirty years after the original John O'Leary Day at the ballpark, I got to celebrate by throwing out the first pitch for the St. Louis Cardinals. My parents were there again to support me, as were my wife and four children.

One of the most generous, positive, and life-affirming
individuals I've ever met is Andre Norman. To consider
the things he once did compared to what he is doing today
should give us all hope that amazing things
remain possible throughout our lives.

Patrick proudly showing the ball
he caught. This is actually the
third ball he has caught at a Major
League Baseball game, because he
always has his glove ready.

Maybe the only creature as naturally In Awe as children are
golden retrievers. Here's our dog, Emma, sharing
a moment of joy with her family.

Patrick, Jack, Grace, and Henry, because of you I am more
daring, loving, and alive. Let this book remind you always
of all you taught me and how much I love you.

Acknowledgments

"What's your favorite thing people say to you after your presentations?"

This was a question someone asked me recently. Without even pausing, I responded immediately: "When someone tells me to go home, hug my wife and kids, and thank them for allowing me to share this message. That's my favorite comment, and it means more than they know."

You see, when I am on the road, in and out of nice hotels, meeting with clients and speaking with audiences, my wife and kids are at home. They make a mighty sacrifice and are the quiet heroes of my story. They are also the inspirations for my work. Beth, I am far more wild about you than I was the day we first met, and am more grateful for you now than at any other point along the journey. You are amazing, and I am the lucky one in our relationship. And to our children, Jack, Patrick, Henry, and Grace: I wrote this book for you, and thank you for your unconditional love, your life-giving lessons, and your contagious joy. Being your dad is the finest job title I possess, and loving you is the greatest joy of my life.

I am aware of no individual who enjoyed finer examples of unconditional love, resolute faith, and purposeful parenting than I received from my parents. Although the odds were less than one in four hundred trillion, I most certainly hit the jackpot in being born their son. Mom and Dad, you were my first and finest teachers. I love you both.

It would have been a very quiet house without my siblings. Jim, Cadey, Amy, Susan, and Laura, thank you for loving me as your little brother, expanding that love during my time of recovery, and persisting in that love over the three decades, many life changes, and ups and downs that have followed. Exploring life with you as kids was awesome. And still is.

Writing a book requires diligent research, significant reflection, heaps of effort, lots of caffeine, and an occasional glass of wine. It also requires a committed team of outstandingly talented individuals guiding the process forward. For us, the team leader is Roger Scholl. He is my editor and advocate with Penguin Random House. Roger saw potential in this book before I even knew what the book was. I met him through Michael Palgon, my magnificent agent and dear friend. He lives in the publishing world, teaches me what I don't know (which is a lot!), doesn't accept good enough as enough, and is the reason my written work continues impacting lives. Cindy DiTiberio is my faithful copilot in the writing process. I would be unfathomably lost in the process of creating a manuscript if it were not for her wisdom, guidance, prodding, and collaboration. Cindy assisted mightily when we wrote *On Fire,* but somehow did an even better job with *In Awe.* These are but a few stars from a publishing team that brought *In Awe* to life. I am beyond grateful for each of them.

And yet, no one would know of this book—or any of my work—if my team didn't do their job with unmatched resolve and commitment. Abby Richter guides forward all of our Live Inspired projects to successful launches. She does an exceptional job of managing the impossibly difficult task of keeping me focused. Abby also leads our team of podcast producers, digital media experts, and business development, marketing, and administrative specialists. It takes a village, and I'm fortunate to be surrounded by, and elevated through, the efforts of a supremely talented team. Sandy Montgomery Schwab,

Aimee Loyet, Heather Arora, and Brian Gaffney are responsible for the impact we have globally. I am grateful for their consistent, unfailing, and unmatched work.

Seven years ago I invited eight business leaders to dream with me about where this business and message could go. My board of advisors is comprised of leaders I look up to professionally, admire personally, and feel connected to spiritually. With little clue as to where this journey would go or what opportunities might be ahead, they agreed to meet with me quarterly, help sharpen my saw, expand the vision, and grow something far bigger than any one person. Thank you, Patrick Barry, Tom Chelew, Dan Curran, Len Dino, Rusty Keeley, Mark LoCigno, Matt Miller, and Matt Rohm.

Two hundred podcast guests. Two thousand corporate clients. A couple million people: readers of my content, those who tuned in at live speaking events, or through the wonder of digital media. A massive list of individuals, by the way, that now includes you, my friend. I am supremely humbled and grateful you've tuned in to this message, are committing to living your life In Awe, and believe, like I do, that your best days remain ahead.

Finally, I am grateful to God for orchestrating this story. For me, I can't fathom calculating the odds of simply being born, the resilience required to endure what I went through as a child, the wondrous collection of individuals who have intersected with my life, the undeserved blessing of Beth's love, or the joy of raising my kids, without seeing God's hand in it. Steve Jobs once spoke about how the ups and downs of life only make sense once we look back on them. That's true. But as I see it, the connector of those dots wasn't me, but the far more wise, loving, and unmitigated power of God. I wake up each day appreciative of grace. It's why I remain grateful for my past, can dance through even difficult days, and remain absolutely confident in my tomorrow.

Notes

INTRODUCTION: RAISE YOUR HAND

1. Brian Resnick, "22 Percent of Millennials Say They Have No Friends," Vox, August 1, 2019.

1: THE PATH OF POSSIBILITY

1. John F. Kennedy, address at Rice University on space exploration, September 12, 1962.

2: WHY?

1. "How Mothers Field 288 Questions a Day," *Daily Mail,* March 28, 2013.
2. "Neil deGrasse Tyson: Kids Are Born Scientists," YouTube video, posted by Monstersnatch, November 22, 2012, at 2:14.
3. Charlotte Alter, "The Young and the Relentless," *Time,* April 2, 2018, 24–31.
4. Warren Berger, "Why Do Kids Ask So Many Questions—And Why Do They Stop?," *A More Beautiful Question* (blog), n.d.
5. George Land and Beth Jarman, *Breaking Point and Beyond* (San Francisco: Harper Business, 1993).
6. Adam Grant, "The Unexpected Sparks of Creativity, Confrontation and Office Culture," *The Goop Podcast,* March 29, 2018.

5: WHAT IF?

1. John O'Leary, "Not Impossible Labs," *Live Inspired with John O'Leary* (podcast), episode 94, August 9, 2018.
2. Alison Gopnik, *The Philosophical Baby: What Children's Minds Tell Us About Truth, Love, and the Meaning of Life* (New York: Picador, 2009), 122.
3. O'Leary, "Not Impossible Labs."

7: BRING YOUR GLOVE

1. Ros Krasny, "Poll: Majority of Americans Say the U.S. Is Headed in the Wrong Direction Under President Trump," *Time,* January 27, 2019.
2. Jamie Ducharme, "A Lot of Americans Are More Anxious Than They Were Last Year, a New Poll Says," *Time,* March 14, 2018.
3. Reuters, "Finland Ranks World's Happiest Country as U.S. Discontent Grows Despite More Riches: UN Report," *South China Morning Post,* March 14, 2018.

8: FIRST-TIME LIVING

1. *City Slickers,* directed by Ron Underwood, screenplay by Lowell Gantz and Babaloo Mandel (Castle Rock Entertainment, 1991).

9: STOP ACTING ORDINARY

1. Ali Binazir, "What Are the Chances You Would Be Born," *Harvard Law Blogs,* June 15, 2011.
2. Huston Smith, *Cleansing the Doors of Perception* (New York: Jeremy P. Tarcher, 2000), 76.

10: LIGHT IT UP

1. John O'Leary, "From Juvie to Jail to Harvard," *Live Inspired with John O'Leary* (podcast), episode 95, August 26, 2018.
2. Ibid.
3. C. R. Snyder et al., "Hope Against the Cold: Individual Differences in Trait Hope and Acute Pain Tolerance on the Cold Pressor Task," *Journal of Personality* 73 (2005): 287–312.
4. K. L. Rand, A. D. Martin, and A. Shea, "Hope, but Not Optimism, Predicts Academic Performance of Law Students Beyond Previous Academic Achievement," *Journal of Research in Personality* 45 (2011): 683–686.
5. S. Stern, R. Dhanda, and H. Hazurda, "Hopelessness Predicts Mortality in Older Mexican and European Americans," *Psychosomatic Medicine* 63 (2001): 344–51.

11: GREAT EXPECTATIONS

1. J. B. Moseley, K. O'Malley, N. J. Petersen, et al., "A Controlled Trial of Arthroscopic Surgery for Osteoarthritis of the Knee," *New England Journal of Medicine* 347, no. 2 (July 11, 2002): 81–88.

2. Michael Pollan, *How to Change Your Mind: What the New Science of Psychedelics Teaches Us About Consciousness, Dying, Addiction, Depression, and Transcendence* (New York: Penguin Books, 2018), 16.

12: THE JOYFUL AWAITING

1. George Loewenstein, "Anticipating the Valuation of Delayed Consumption," *Economic Journal* 97, no. 387 (September 1987): 666–684.

14: FUTURE FOCUS

1. Josh Moody, "Where the Top Fortune 500 CEOs Attended College," *US News and World Report,* June 11, 2019.

15: WORK. PLAY. REST. REPEAT.

1. Daniel Levitin, *The Organized Mind: Thinking Straight in the Age of Information Overload* (New York: Dutton, 2015), 98.

2. Larry Kim, "Multitasking Is Killing Your Brain," *Inc.,* July 15, 2015.

3. Alex Cocotas, "88% of U.S. Consumers Use Mobile as Second Screen While Watching TV," *Business Insider,* May 20, 2013.

16: HANG IT ON THE FRIDGE

1. Ed O'Boyle and Annamarie Mann, "American Workplace Changing at Dizzying Pace," Gallup Workplace, February 15, 2017, www.gallup.com/workplace /236282/american-workplace-changing-dizzying-pace.aspx.

2. Martin Luther King Jr., "The Three Dimensions of a Complete Life," sermon delivered at the Unitarian Church of Germantown, kinginstitute.stanford .edu/king-papers/documents/three-dimensions-complete-life-sermon-delivered -unitarian-church-germantown.

3. Charles Duhigg, "Wealthy, Successful and Miserable," *New York Times Magazine,* February 24, 2019, 26.

4. Nathan Zeldes, " 'Quiet Time' and 'No Email Day' Pilot Data Is In!," Intel IT Peer Network, June 14, 2008, itpeernetwork.intel.com/quiet-time-and-no -email-day-pilot-data-is-in/#gs.fgis24.

5. Adam Grant, "When Work Takes Over Your Life," *Work Life with Adam Grant* (podcast), April 17, 2018.

17: GO FLY A KITE

1. Sara Burrows, "Texas School Beats ADHD by Tripling Recess Time," *Return to Now* (blog), November 21, 2017.
2. Ibid.
3. David Epstein, *Range: Why Generalists Triumph in a Specialized World* (New York: Riverhead Books, 2019).
4. Steven Kotler, "Flow States and Creativity," *Psychology Today*, February 25, 2014.
5. Doris Kearns Goodwin, *Team of Rivals: The Political Genius of Abraham Lincoln* (New York: Simon & Schuster, 2005), 609.
6. Lily Rothman, "Historian Doris Kearns Goodwin Looks to Past Leaders for Lessons on the Present," *Time*, September 17, 2018, 12–13.

18: LOOK UP AT THE CLOUDS

1. Florence Williams, *The Nature Fix: Why Nature Makes Us Happier, Healthier, and More Creative* (New York: W. W. Norton, 2017), 49.
2. Oliver Sacks, *Everything in Its Place: First Loves and Last Tales* (London: Picador, 2019).
3. Williams, *The Nature Fix*, 23.
4. Jamie Ducharme, "Spending Just 20 Minutes in a Park Makes You Happier," *Time*, February 28, 2019.
5. Tony Schwartz, "Relax! You'll Be More Productive," *New York Times*, February 10, 2013.
6. Tony Schwartz, *The Way We're Working Isn't Working: The Four Forgotten Needs That Energize Great Performance* (New York: Simon & Schuster, 2010).
7. Judith Shulevitz, "Bring Back the Sabbath," *New York Times Magazine*, February 3, 2003. www.nytimes.com/2003/03/02/magazine/bring-back-the-sabbath.html.
8. Patricia Hampl, "Baby Boomers Reach the End of Their To-Do List," *New York Times*, April 14, 2018.

19: IT'S YOUR JOB

1. Mitch Albom, "Chika's Story," *Detroit Free Press*, June 11, 2017.
2. Richard Harris, "The Moment That Changed Mitch Albom's Life," *Forbes*, March 29, 2017.

20: WHAT TIME IS IT?

1. William James, *The Principles of Psychology* (New York: Henry Holt, 1890), 260.

22: THE CONTAGION OF JOY

1. Robert Firestone, Lisa A. Firestone, and Joyce Catlett, *The Self Under Siege: A Therapeutic Model for Differentiation* (New York and London: Routledge, 2013), 206.
2. Nicholas A. Christakis and James H. Fowler, "Dynamic Spread of Happiness in a Large Social Network," *British Medical Journal,* December 5, 2008.
3. Daniel Goleman, "The Experience of Touch," *New York Times,* February 2, 1988.
4. Benedict Carey, "Evidence That Little Touches Do Mean So Much," *New York Times,* February 22, 2010.

23: A PIECE OF THE PUZZLE

1. Dan Buettner, *The Blue Zones of Happiness: Lessons from the World's Happiest People* (Washington, DC: National Geographic, 2017), 173.
2. Ibid.

24: STOP HIDING IN THE SHADOWS

1. John O'Leary, "Dare to Lead," *Live Inspired with John O'Leary* (podcast), episode 103, October 11, 2018.

25: JOIN THE PARTY

1. Thomas Merton, *No Man Is an Island* (Boston: Shambhala, 2005), 177.
2. John O'Leary, "Demystifying Disabilities," *Live Inspired with John O'Leary* (podcast), episode 85, June 7, 2018.
3. John Zarocostas, "Disabled Still Face Hurdles in Job Market," *Washington Times,* December 4, 2005.
4. Melonyce McAfee, "Advocate for Disabled Workers Is 2017 CNN Hero of the Year," CNN, March 8, 2018.
5. Ibid.
6. Ibid.
7. Meik Wiking, *The Little Book of Lykke: Secrets of the World's Happiest People* (New York: William Morrow, 2017), 201.

27: PLAY TO WIN

1. Leslie Kendall Dye, "Dear Strangers, Please Stop Telling Me My Active Daughter Might Get Hurt," *Washington Post,* November 1, 2016.
2. Lauren Knight, "5 Ways to Let a Little More Risk into Your Child's Day," *Washington Post,* January 16, 2015.
3. Peter Gray, "Risky Play: Why Children Love It and Need It," *Psychology Today,* April 7, 2014.

29: SING OUT LOUD

1. "Bullying Definition, Statistics and Risk Factors," American Society for the Positive Care of Children, americanspcc.org/our-voice/bullying/statistics-and-information.
2. Oliver Wendell Holmes, *Elsie Venner: A Romance of Destiny* (Boston and New York: Houghton, Mifflin and Company, 1861), 10.

EPILOGUE: AWESTRUCK

1. Carl Sagan, *Pale Blue Dot: A Vision of the Human Future in Space* (New York: Random House, 1994), 6.

Index

About the Author

Once expected to die young, JOHN O'LEARY now teaches others how to truly live. As an internationally acclaimed speaker, bestselling author, and renowned podcast host, John helps hundreds of thousands of people each year to live inspired, sharing his insights and uplifting message with emotional storytelling and unexpected humor. In a marketplace and media climate that often feels negative, John created his Live Inspired media channel to share the other side of the story, utilizing his Monday Motivation essays, *Live Inspired Podcast,* and more, to "do life" with his online community of three hundred thousand friends. He's the author of the #1 national bestseller *On Fire* and lives with his wife and their four children in St. Louis, Missouri.

About the Type

This book was set in Bembo, a typeface based on an old-style Roman face that was used for Cardinal Pietro Bembo's tract *De Aetna* in 1495. Bembo was cut by Francesco Griffo (1450–1518) in the early sixteenth century for Italian Renaissance printer and publisher Aldus Manutius (1449–1515). The Lanston Monotype Company of Philadelphia brought the well-proportioned letterforms of Bembo to the United States in the 1930s.

"THIS IS A BOOK ABOUT COMING ALIVE—
about practicing courage and fully showing up at home,
work, and with the people we love. John is a storyteller,
change-maker, and cage-rattler. Reading this book
is like having a good friend look you square in the
eye and say, 'The time to be brave is now.'"

—BRENÉ BROWN, Ph.D., LMSW, #1 *New York Times* bestselling
author of *Daring Greatly* and *Rising Strong*

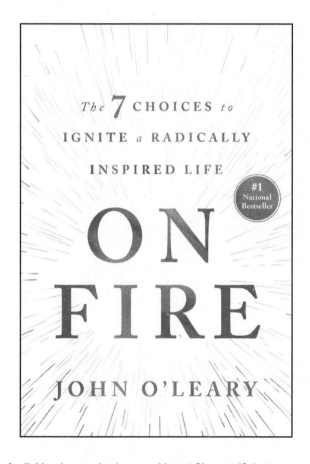

Available wherever books are sold or at SimonandSchuster.com

GALLERY BOOKS